On January 15, 1997,

the Belleview Mido Resort Hotel

will celebrate its centennial anniversary.

No such celebration could be considered complete

without taking time to reflect on the proud tradition of this landmark

and to pay tribute to the notable and colorful cast of characters

who have brought us to where we are today.

It is with this goal in mind that we are pleased

to make this pictorial history available,

recognizing our responsibility to preserve this legacy

as we continue this exciting journey.

Hideo Kurosawa
Owner

Jeffry Martin
General Manager

The Belleview Mido Resort Hotel

A Century of Hospitality

By
Prudy Taylor Board
& Esther B. Colcord

THE
DONNING COMPANY
PUBLISHERS

Copyright © 1996 by Prudy Taylor Board and Esther B. Colcord
All rights reserved, including the right to reproduce this work in any form whatsoever without permission in writing from the publisher, except for brief passages in connection with a review.
For information, write:
The Donning Company/Publishers
184 Business Park Drive, Suite 106
Virginia Beach, VA 23462

Steve Mull, General Manager
B. L. Walton Jr., Project Director
Laura D. Hill, Project Research Coordinator
Richard A. Horwege, Editor
Cynthia Dooley, Graphic Designer
Dawn V. Kofroth, Production Manager
Tony Lillis, Director of Marketing
Teri S. Arnold, Marketing Assistant

Library of Congress Cataloging-in-Publication Data

Board, Prudy Taylor, 1933–
    The Belleview Mido Resort Hotel : a century of hospitality / by Prudy Taylor Board and Esther B. Colcord.
        p.   cm.
    Includes bibliographical references and index.
    ISBN 0-89865-981-7 (hc : alk. paper)
    1. Belleview Mido Resort Hotel (Clearwater, Fla.) 2. Hotels—Florida—
       Clearwater—History. I. Colcord, Esther B. II. Title.

TX941.B45B63   1996
647.94759'6501—dc20   96-43081
                                                                     CIP

Printed in the United States of America

Contents

Foreword
Page 7

Acknowledgments
Page 9

CHAPTER ONE
1897–1919
Page 10

CHAPTER TWO
1919–1945
Page 32

CHAPTER THREE
1946–1972
Page 58

CHAPTER FOUR
1973–1997
Page 82

CHAPTER FIVE
Through the Years in Color
Page 106

Bibliography
Page 124

Index
Page 126

About the Authors
Page 128

Foreword

One hundred years ago on January 15, 1897, the Belleview opened its doors and its 145 rooms to a gathering of founder and transportation magnate Henry B. Plant's friends, family, and business associates. Also at this gathering was a host of area residents who had watched in wonder, during the previous eighteen months as the magnificent structure that would soon become known as "The White Queen of the Gulf" took shape, high above the Intracoastal Waterways of Clearwater.

From this moment, the west coast of Florida was assured a prominent place on the map, as well as in the hearts and minds of many of the world's most seasoned travelers, and our area's position as a leading destination was secured. It is certainly not too much to say that the growth and success of this legendary landmark and its surrounding communities have been inexorably linked ever since, each nourishing and nurturing the other, their histories and prosperity unfolding almost as one.

In fact, the entire state of Florida has benefited enormously from the attention this resort has received, the friends it has made, and the gracious hospitality it has bestowed over the years. At a time when many have lamented the previous lack of attention paid to our colorful and unique history, and accurately noted the growing desire among travelers for attractions and experiences that lend themselves to learning as well as to simply relaxing, we are especially proud and grateful that this special structure remains with us, beautifully preserved, restored, and expanded. Its historical significance was officially recognized in 1979 when the Belleview was listed on the National Register of Historic Places.

Landmarks such as this deserve our attention and respect. The window they provide to our past, and the perspective they add to our current outlook and activities is extraordinary. This legacy is priceless, the contribution to our heritage truly unique. We are proud of the role that the Belleview and its people have played in our past, eager to watch its continued impact on our future, and with great pride recommend this tribute to you.

Governor Lawton Chiles

Mayor Rita Garvey of Clearwater

Mayor Stephen G. Watts of Belleair

U.S. Senator Connie Mack

U.S. Senator Bob Graham

Congressman C.W. Bill Young

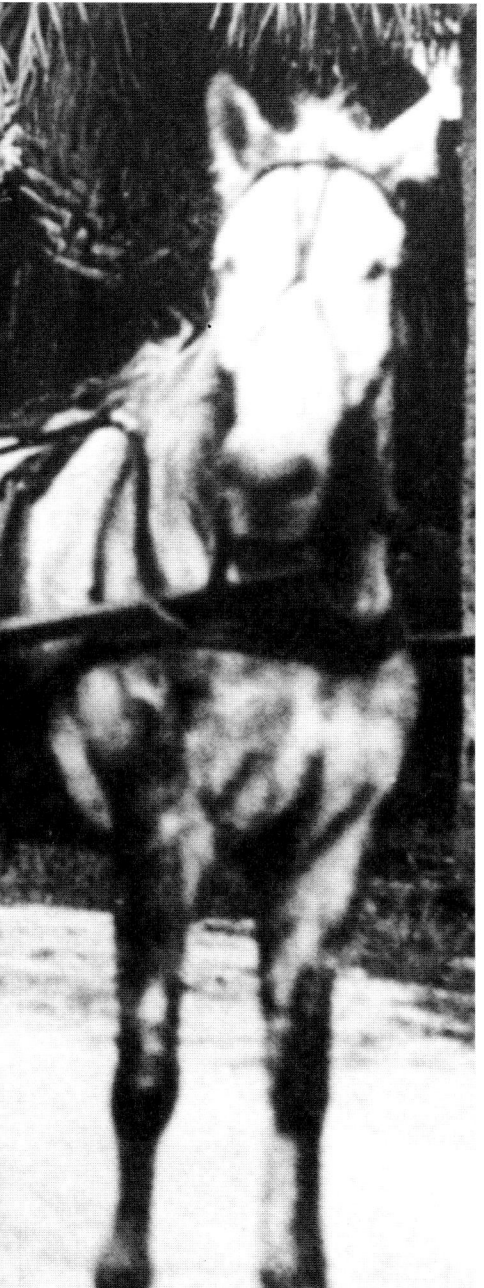

Acknowledgments

The complete list of people from whom we received help would take far too much space. Most people, in fact, didn't necessarily want credit—they just wanted us to write a good book, an accurate history and they were willing to do what they could to help. To all of those kind people, we say thank you. We sincerely appreciate not only your assistance and your time, but your hospitality. Special folks who went above and beyond the call of duty include Kathy Powell Strong; Belleview Mido General Manager Jeff Martin; Maintenance Supervisor Gary Larson; Marketing Coordinator Karin Case; Director of Sales and Marketing Oliver Kugler; Tour Guides Patricia Counts and Trudy Miller; Conference Services Manager Todd Dixon; Flo Zimmerman, the *Bellair Bee's* splendid photographer; Belleair Town Clerk Lorain Blankenship; Fire Chief Robin Millican; Don Ivey from Heritage Village; Melinda Chavez; Curator Susan Carter and Linda Plumb from the Henry B. Plant Museum in Tampa; Mike Morris and Fireman Chris Sipiora who knew more about the fire truck than the manufacturer; Joan Morris at the Florida State Photo Archives; Becky Hill of the Historical Association of Southern Florida; Strawberry Luck, photo archivist at Vanderbilt University; William McKenzie Woodward, Architectural Historian, Historical Preservation, State of Rhode Island; Mildred Santiago and Stan Mulford from the Fort Myers Historical Museum; Dave McKelvey, General Manager of WZVN-TV, the ABC affiliate in Fort Myers; the Donald J. Ross Foundation and Museum; and Charles Risher and Cathleen Baldwin of the Biltmore Estate in Asheville, North Carolina.

These dapper champion bicyclists were members of the Eldredge Cycle Club in England. They had come to race on the Belleview Hotel's internationally acclaimed quarter-mile-long bicycle track. (Photo from the Belleview Mido Collection)

CHAPTER ONE

1897–1919

Facing page: In 1896, these construction workers operated mule-powered scrapers as they graded the area around the 145-room hotel. Heart of pine lumber from South Georgia and North Florida was used for structural timbers. The wood, nearly impervious to termites, is also virtually uninflammable. When constructed, the hotel was four stories high, ran four hundred feet from east to west and was ninety-six feet wide. (Photo from the Belleview Mido Collection)

Below: The Belleview bicycle track which included a grandstand for viewing was also used for horse racing during the 1898–99 tourist season. The bicycle track has been described as wooden, asphalt, and even brick. However, the Pinellas County Historical Museum lays claim to a section of the old bicycle path which is actually constructed of oyster shell. It was demolished between 1910 and 1914 to build one of the golf courses. (Photo from the Belleview Mido Collection)

Like a genteel Southern grande dame, the Belleview stands poised as she has for a century, ready to welcome and dispense hospitality to her guests. Dubbed "The White Queen of the Gulf," the Belleview Mido is impressive for many reasons:
- she is reportedly the largest occupied wooden structure in the world;
- her corridors stretch two miles and carpeting is purchased by the mile not the square yard;
- before the aluminum siding was installed in 1975, one thousand gallons were required to paint this elegant lady.

These stark statistics don't even hint at the Belleview Mido's dizzying saga, a fascinating history which spans a century, a journal that glitters with the names of the wealthiest, most renowned citizens of our country.

The Belleview, brainchild of transportation magnate Henry B. Plant, was destined for success from the day her doors were opened. A Connecticut Yankee, Plant had arrived in Florida in early April 1853 accompanied by his wife and son, Morton. The family's move from New York was motivated by Ellen Plant's illness, she had contracted tuberculosis.

Her health, nurtured by Florida's benign weather, improved greatly and the Plants returned to New York in the spring. When the consumption recurred the following winter, the Plants returned to Florida. Accepting the inevitable, Plant accepted a job as superintendent of Adams Express' Southern division in 1854.

When the War between the States erupted in 1861 jeopardizing the Southern division, Plant convinced Adams' management to sell him their Southern operations which he incorporated as the Southern Express Company and his journey to incredible wealth and success was launched.

Plant's triumph was bittersweet and marred by tragedy for Ellen Plant succumbed during the winter of 1862 and was buried in Augusta, Georgia. Following the war, he took her remains back to Branford, Connecticut, where she is buried in the Center Cemetery. After her death, Plant immersed himself in work to such an extent that he nearly died. Acting on his doctor's advice,

Left: The beautiful, wood-paneled Belleview lobby in the early 1900s was large enough (fifty-two by sixty-five feet) to hold the house orchestra that often played for the guests as they waited to check in for the winter season. The area was highlighted by a grand staircase, fan light windows, and a fourteen-foot high ceiling. One of the architectural marvels was the suspended ceiling constructed with several arches, each arch containing ten segments of laminated wood. The weight of the ceiling and upper floors is supported by a plethora of one-and-one-half-inch rods that hang from the arches and, hidden within the walls, extend from the ground floor to the roof. (Photo from the Ullman Collection)

Right: Henry B. Plant connected short line railroads in South Carolina, Georgia, Alabama, and Florida; standardized the gauge; and developed "The Plant System." In so doing, he opened central and western Florida to phenomenal growth. (Photo courtesy of the Henry B. Plant Museum Archives, Tampa, Florida)

Above: Golf was important to the Belleview from the beginning, but even more so once Morton F. Plant became vice president of the Plant Investment Company. In this photo taken around the turn of the century, hotel guests watched an ardent golfer tee off on the first tee of the hotel's six-hole golf course with shell greens. The small sign reads "262 yards." Brochures advertised "six sporty holes of golf." (Photo from the Belleview Mido Collection)

he turned management of his business over to his staff and spent a year recuperating in Europe and coping with his grief. When Robert E. Lee surrendered at Appomattox marking the end of the war, Plant returned bearing Northern money that enabled him to buy up bankrupt Southern railroads, solidifying his fortune.

In the years that followed, Plant developed a transportation system that included steamships as well as railroads. In Florida, his trains ran from Tampa to Jacksonville and thence to Savannah and Charleston, South Carolina; his ships from Tampa to Key West and Havana.

Not content with dominating the transportation industry in West Florida, Plant decided to build or acquire a series of luxury hotels as destinations for the passengers who traveled to Florida on vacation via his trains. And, taking his dream one step further, he planned communities such as Belleair in the vicinity of his resorts.

Although Florida was still a wilderness frontier, the development of the area surrounding the Belleview had gotten a boost in 1870. Charles Wharton Johnson, owner and captain of an eight-ton sailing vessel named *Evening Star*, made regular trips from Cedar Key to Fort Myers carrying mail, freight, and infrequent passengers. On one of his journeys, he sighted the long, high ridge where the Belleview is located and decided to explore the area. He did and in 1870, he moved his family, built a home, and planted a citrus grove on the land. When the grove failed, Johnson moved family and grove to Largo, Florida.

By the early 1890s, Plant's agents were quietly scouting locations for a luxury resort. Plant was as intrigued by the site as Captain Johnson had been and bought the property. The real estate broker was J. J. Eldridge and Plant was apparently so pleased with Eldridge that he hired him first as paymaster, then as the Belleview's construction superintendent. Eldridge also is said to have designed the Belleview's first six-hole golf course. Plant commissioned Tampa architects Michael J. Miller and Francis J. Kennard to design the hotel; his associate J. W. Newman surveyed the land surrounding the hotel and laid out a new town to be called Belleair. The first houses in the town were built by Belleview guests who wanted to come earlier and stay later than the season. The houses that remain are still considered some of the most attractive to be found in the area.

During the summer of 1895, an army of three hundred laborers moved into the area and began clearing the land. That same year Plant bought the Orange Belt Railroad, made a standard gauge road, and built a depot on Cleveland Street.

The Belleview opened on January 15, 1897, with 145 rooms. "Every

Left: W. J. Fleming, Belleview manager, published this brochure in 1908, citing not only the golf links, turf putting greens, and tees but also the excellent fishing, swimming, cycling, and even a visit to Seminole shell mounds where Indian artifacts might be found. (Photo from the Ullman Collection)

Above: The Belleview reputedly hosted more corporate and railroad executives than any other resort in America. As many as fifteen private Pullman cars were sometimes parked at one time on the hotel's special siding while their executives were guests. During the winter of 1912, a car was parked on the special siding and equipped as a hospital. Henry Plant II had been thrown from an automobile on the road between Clearwater and St. Petersburg. His hip and leg were badly injured by the car's chain drive. Morton Plant, distressed by the lack of hospital facilities, ordered a railroad car staffed with the best doctor, nurses, and equipment sent from Chicago. Young Henry spent three months recuperating in the rail car and Morton donated money to help build what is now known as the Morton F. Plant Hospital. (Photo from the Belleview Mido Collection)

Above: In August 1896, a Tampa Weekly Tribune *reporter enthusiastically opined, "Messrs. Michael Miller and Francis J. Kennard, the architects of this wonderful creation, must have long courted the muses in their effort to reach perfection." Large verandahs, ten feet wide on either side of the entrance, were a popular gathering place for guests. From the verandahs, guests could enjoy a view of the beautiful Clearwater Bay. (Photo from the Belleview Mido Collection)*

Right: In 1878, Plant married Margaret Josephine Loughman of New York. His first wife, Ellen Elizabeth Blackstone, had died in 1861. An assertive woman, his second wife successfully sued Plant's estate after his death. Although he had wanted the majority of his holdings held in trust for a grandson, Margaret broke the trust in court and his railroads were sold off to Atlantic Coast Line Railroad. (Photo courtesy of Henry B. Plant Museum Archives, Tampa, Florida)

Below: Henry Bradley Plant, born in Branford, Connecticut, on October 27, 1819, was described as the man who "introduced railroads, built steamships, laid out towns and erected hotels, and through it all, his judgment never failed him." His family had little money, but was composed of respectable farmers who could trace their ancestry in Connecticut back to 1677. Plant didn't finish high school and spent five years as a deckhand before his vision and determination transformed him into the transportation tycoon and developer who forever changed the face of Southwest Florida. (Photo courtesy of the Henry B. Plant Museum Archives, Tampa, Florida)

Below: The entrance bridge, as shown in this photo circa 1900, provided much more than access to the hotel. It housed a curio shop, antique shop, and two museums—one exhibiting mounted fish and the other mounted animals. (Photo courtesy of Florida State Archives)

Above Left: The boat dock and bathing pavilion were popular with guests. Boats were available for fishing, sightseeing, and transportation to and from Sand Key Beach. (Photo from the Belleview Mido Collection)

Above Right: Donald J. Ross, renowned golf course designer, was famous for his innovative hazards. In some cases, like the Belleview west course, he used a raised tee so the golfer could observe the hazard before he hit the ball. Ross has been credited with more than 412 course designs. (Photo courtesy of the Donald Ross Foundation)

Left: In the early 1900s, the horse and carriage was a popular mode of transportation around the Belleview. Riding in the carriage is young Ray E. Green, who first served as mayor of Clearwater from 1936 to 1938 and as Florida state comptroller from 1955 to 1965. (Photo courtesy of Heritage Village)

Plant acquired this home in Clearwater in 1896 when his Orange Belt Railroad was completed. Originally the site was homesteaded in 1875. Known today as the Henry B. Plant House, it has been preserved and is considered historically significant because of its simplicity in design and because much of the original molding, trim, and windows remains. (Sketch courtesy of Heritage Village)

bedroom has three incandescent lights" reported a brochure written for the 1898 season, in addition to "a mantel of polished cedar with handsome tiling surrounding the fireplace, polished floors and oak or cherry furniture. There are several suites of rooms with bath connected." Telegraph, telephone, and newsstand were inside the hotel where the shops are today because Plant was well aware of how important it was guests be able to stay informed and in touch with their offices. A barber shop and billiards were available in the basement. A livery stable was connected to the hotel and operated until 1950 when it was no longer profitable.

Guests were entertained by daily concerts performed by a house orchestra, but there were many other activities—golfing, bicycle racing, hunting, fishing, horseback riding, yachting, skeetshooting, and tennis.

Plant was not to enjoy his achievement long. He died suddenly on June 23, 1899, at his Fifth Avenue home in New York City. His son, Morton, took over as vice president of the Plant Investment Company and ran the Belleview until his death in 1918.

One of Morton's first contributions to the hotel was the decision to paint the original wood exterior, which had faded to a dull color, a bright white and retile the roof with green shingles (instead of red) in the early 1900s. The Belleview then became known as the "White Queen of The Gulf."

An interesting sidelight to the year 1918 was the formation of the Stone Crab Club. Its membership consisted of guests who had spent at least five winters at the Belleview. Members were given a silver buckle in the shape of a crab; at the annual party, stone crabs and champagne were always served.

Under Morton Plant's leadership, the hotel prospered. In 1910, the east wing was added doubling the hotel's capacity. In 1915, he hired Donald J. Ross to design two golf courses and, even though it was commonly believed that grasses for greens wouldn't grow in Florida, Plant experimented with grasses, fertilizers, and soils. He even brought trainloads of topsoil from Indiana and accomplished his goal—grass greens. The golf courses played a major role in the hotel's success for they drew the country's most prominent professional and amateur golfers.

It was also during Morton Plant's regime that *Palm Cottage* was built in 1900 as the first in a series of private winter homes constructed on the hotel grounds for wealthy families.

In 1914, after the automobile accident involving young Henry Plant II, Morton Plant offered an endowment fund of $100,000 for maintenance of a hospital in Clearwater. Morton Plant Hospital opened in 1916 with twenty-one rooms.

Facing page: These young couples enjoying a "bicycle break" in the early 1900s included Miss Dickie McKenzie and Nick Butler, the hotel water supervisor (top); Miss Hallie Ziegler and unidentifed (standing); and left to right, Miss Flossie Rogers (seated), evangelist Reverend Ed Culpepper (seated), and George Bolton (standing). The cyclists had probably just finished the five-mile ride through the surrounding citrus groves enjoying the beauty of exotic trees such as orchid, bottlebrush, Florida holly, and jacarandas. (Photo courtesy of Florida State Archives)

Above: The landscape was barren of any trace of civilization—other than the hotel—when the Belleview was finally completed. However, it was the wilderness ambiance, the jungle outpost atmosphere that lured the questing jet set from the comfortable surroundings of the big cities. (Photo from the Belleview Mido Collection)

Below: By late 1896, the hotel was completed, but the landscaping had not matured as this photo shows. On January 15, 1897, when the hotel opened, however, the hotel was such a success few noticed. (Photo from the Belleview Mido Collection)

In 1917, at his wife's urging, construction began on an Olympic-sized swimming pool. Dedicated as always to excellence, Plant brought tile setters from Italy to install the more than one million multicolored ceramic tiles which lined the seventy-five-by-sixty-foot pool.

Following Morton Plant's death, the Belleview changed hands. Purchased by John McEntee Bowman of the Biltmore Hotel chain in 1919, the hotel, now known as the Belleview Biltmore, looked confidently toward a promising future.

Above: Donald Ross, born in Dornoch, Scotland, came to America in 1899 at twenty-seven and took the job of golf pro at the Oakley Country Club in Massachusetts. As a golfer, he won the Massachusetts Open, the North-South Open, and placed well in the U.S. National and the British Championship Opens. The two eighteen-hole golf courses he designed on the Belleview property attracted golfing greats including Bobby Jones, Irvin S. Cobb, George Ade, Babe Ruth, and Judge Kennesaw Mountain Landis. Babe Didrickson, a world-famous female American athlete, also enjoyed the Belleview courses. In fact, the golf courses played a vital role in the success of the hotel. (Photo courtesy of The Donald Ross Foundation)

Left: These young women didn't appear to be hampered by their long skirts as they played doubles on the hotel tennis court around the turn of the century. The Belleview offered a number of pastimes—fishing, hunting, croquet, tennis, golf, and concerts. (Photo from the Belleview Mido Collection)

Right: The S.S. Mascotte *and* S.S. Olivette, *vessels on the roster of the Plant steamship line, sailed from Tampa to Key West to Havana carrying U.S. mail, passengers, and freight. They also transported wounded and sick soldiers and refugees from Cuba during the Spanish-American War. (Photo courtesy of the Henry B. Plant Museum Archives, Tampa, Florida)*

Below: In 1910 another army of laborers was hired and the 120-foot east wing was added, doubling the size and capacity of the hotel. A new, much larger kitchen and dining room were established on the north side of the main wing. (Photo from the Belleview Mido Collection)

*The northwest lawn of the Belleview grounds.
(Photo from the Belleview Mido Collection)*

This 1914 luncheon menu is evidence that fine food was an important consideration at the Belleview from its inception. (Photo from the Belleview Mido Collection)

Today's connoisseurs of fine wines and liqueurs will be amazed at the prices on this 1901 wine list. (Photo from the Belleview Mido Collection)

Right: After Henry Plant's death, his son, Morton Freeman Plant, became vice president. One of his early projects was the repainting of the hotel. Originally the roof was red and the hotel was brown, but Morton had the roof painted green and the hotel white, colors which have become the hotel's trademark. The son had a passion for golf and added two eighteen-hole golf courses and, at the urging of his wife, a large swimming pool. The hotel thrived for the next twenty years under Morton's guidance and the east wing was added doubling the size of occupancy from 145 to 290 guest rooms. (Photo courtesy of the Henry B. Plant Museum Archives, Tampa, Florida)

Childrens Sand Box, Belleair, Fla.

Left: The Belleview Hotel was never insensitive to children's needs. These children, dressed rather formally for play in the sandbox, do look so well behaved they appear almost somber. (Photo courtesy of Heritage Village)

Above: For many years, the Belleview Hotel owned this 1917 American LaFrance fire engine. The Belleview was also probably one of the earliest hotels to have its own fire department and police force. Purchased new in 1917, "Frances" was top of the line. She had a thirty-foot extension ladder, a searchlight, locomotive bell with a clapper, an electric siren horn, and pumped 375 gallons of water per minute. In 1927, the town of Belleair agreed to pay $35 a month toward the fire chief's salary and truck repairs. The hotel provided housing for the chief and the truck and paid the insurance. She was stationed at the Belleview until 1934 when she was given to the Belleair Fire Department. In 1964, she was sold to the Largo Lions Club. (Photo courtesy of Chris Sipiora and the Belleair Fire Department)

Above: This announcement marking the opening of the 1898 winter season features cyclists on a path flanked by cabbage palms with Clearwater Bay in the background—an irresistible combination to entice the rich and famous from the North. (Photo from the Belleview Mido Collection)

Left: Watched by friends and admirers, Henry B. Plant teed off, on the new nine-hole golf course with sand greens designed and constructed in 1899 by Launcelot Cressy Servos. (Photo courtesy of Heritage Village)

Below: The Belleview Hotel proved an ideal vacation spot for industry leaders such as Thomas Edison (right), inventor among other things of the light bulb, moving pictures, and stock market ticker. His son and Henry Ford (left), the auto manufacturer, often accompanied him. Ford, although on vacation, had to be in constant contact with his plants in Detroit so the Belleview was an excellent choice. Wireless, telephone, and telegraph services were available on the premises as well as a post office. Guests could even buy the Wall Street Journal and keep up with the stock market. (Photo courtesy of Fort Myers Historical Museum)

Right: Although this composition never made the Top Ten, the Belleview was one of the few hotels to have a waltz composed in its honor. Actually, Plant commissioned Miss Stella Spurlin of Camden, Alabama, to compose "The Belleview Waltz" which was dedicated to Mrs. H. B. Plant. (Courtesy of the Henry B. Plant Museum Archives, Tampa, Florida)

In 1828, when Henry Plant was nine, only 3 miles of railroad track existed in the entire nation. By the time of his death on June 23, 1899, he controlled 2,139 miles of railroad track and owned seven coastal steamship lines. In 1901 when the Plant System was sold, the railroad was valued at $7,475,883 and paid a total of $132,770 in state and county taxes. During the 1880s and 1890s, despite the economic recession and severe freezes that plagued the 1890s, the Plant System prospered paying dividends to stockholders while other transportation companies were folding. (Map courtesy of the Henry B. Plant Museum Archives, Tampa, Florida)

Right: In 1916, Morton refused to buy Maisie a string of perfectly matched Oriental pearls from Cartier's saying that at $1.2 million the necklace was too expensive. Not to be outdone, Maisie bargained with Pierre Cartier and traded her wedding present, the Plant mansion on Fifth Avenue in New York City where they had lived fifteen years. The House of Cartier is still open at that location. Cartier's illustrated the story in their 1994 catalogue, as pictured here, by contrasting the building with a 54-inch strand of 9-9-1/2 mm. cultured pearls with a pavé diamond clasp set in 18K white gold. (Courtesy of the Henry B. Plant Museum Archives, Tampa, Florida)

Left: When widower Morton Plant met then married Maisie Cadwell Manwaring, he was so bewitched he offered her husband $8 million to divorce her. It was, obviously, an offer too good to refuse for Maisie soon became Maisie Manwaring Plant and Morton gained custody of her son, Philip, whom he later adopted. (Courtesy of the Henry B. Plant Museum Archives, Tampa, Florida)

The Plant insignia became prominent throughout Southwest Florida as Plant expanded his business holdings from railroads to steamship lines and then hotels. According to research from the Henry B. Plant Museum, when Plant's estate—valued between $40 and $70 million—was liquidated, the railway properties became part of the Atlantic Coast Line (now CSX) and most of the steamship properties went to the Peninsular and Occidental Steamship Company. The Southern Express Company became the now defunct Railway Express Company. Of the eight hotels, only the Belleview is still operated as a hotel. (Photo courtesy of the Henry B. Plant Museum Archives, Tampa, Florida)

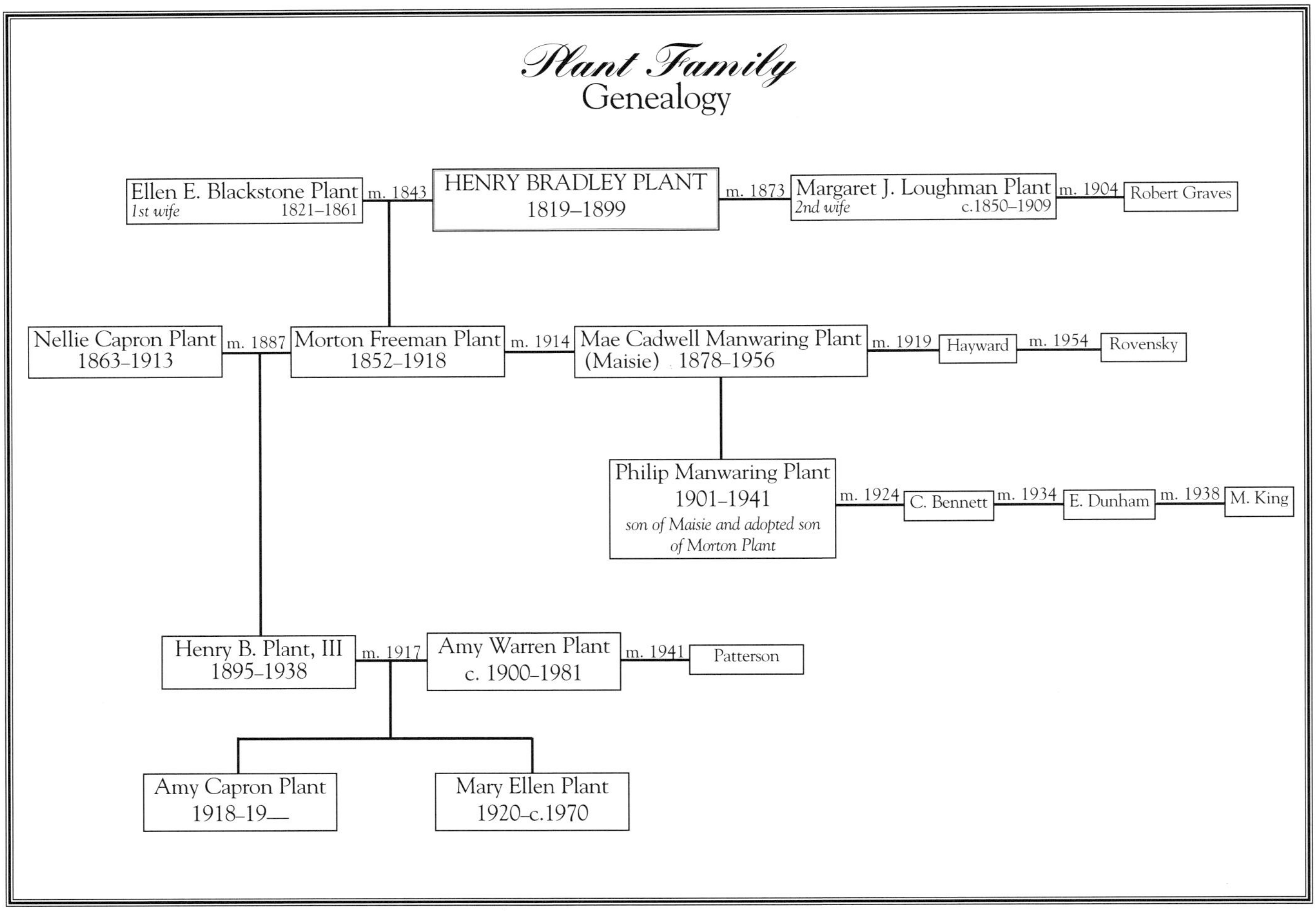

Plant Family Genealogy

Ellen E. Blackstone Plant, 1st wife, 1821–1861 — m. 1843 — **HENRY BRADLEY PLANT** 1819–1899 — m. 1873 — Margaret J. Loughman Plant, 2nd wife, c.1850–1909 — m. 1904 — Robert Graves

Nellie Capron Plant 1863–1913 — m. 1887 — Morton Freeman Plant 1852–1918 — m. 1914 — Mae Cadwell Manwaring Plant (Maisie) 1878–1956 — m. 1919 — Hayward — m. 1954 — Rovensky

Philip Manwaring Plant 1901–1941, *son of Maisie and adopted son of Morton Plant* — m. 1924 — C. Bennett — m. 1934 — E. Dunham — m. 1938 — M. King

Henry B. Plant, III 1895–1938 — m. 1917 — Amy Warren Plant c. 1900–1981 — m. 1941 — Patterson

Amy Capron Plant 1918–19—

Mary Ellen Plant 1920–c.1970

Henry B. Plant's Family Genealogy.

Above: A geological oddity, this fresh water spring in the middle of a body of salt water supplied the hotel's drinking water which was piped into the hotel. Soft lake water was used for bathing and other purposes. (Photo from the Belleview Mido Collection)

Right: The main entrance about 1897. (Photo from the Belleview Mido Collection)

In the 1930s, these wise guests protected themselves from Florida's blazing sun by hiding beneath hats and umbrellas while playing bridge and writing notes back to their friends in the frozen North. (Photo from the Belleview Mido Collection)

CHAPTER

1919–1945

Two

As the second decade of the new century began, Americans were ecstatic. World War I had ended in 1918, the victorious soldiers had returned home and the country was abrim with enthusiasm and energy as it adjusted to peacetime. The Belleview was also in a period of adjustment for John McEntee Bowman of the Biltmore Hotel chain had purchased the hotel in 1919 from the Plant Investment Company following Morton Plant's death.

The name *Biltmore* was added in 1919 and in 1924 the second and final addition was begun. When completed, the hotel had 425 rooms; of these, 380 were guest rooms. The rest were used for staff and administrative purposes. James H. Ritchie of Brookline, Massachusetts, was the architect for this $1 million expansion which included the construction of the south wing and an addition to the dormitory as well as enlarging the grand dining room, the Tiffany Room.

The 1920s were giddy, exhilarating times and the Belleview Biltmore and its roster of guests reflected the aura of extravagance and indulgence. The railroad presidents pulled up on the Belleview Biltmore's siding in their private cars. The Studebakers, the DuPonts, the Pew family of Sun Oil, the Vanderbilts—America's aristocracy—checked in. In 1920, the Olympic pool that had been Mrs. Morton Plant's pride was used for Olympic swimming trials. The Belleview Biltmore golf links were peopled by some of the most famous golfers and athletes in the country—Babe Ruth, Bobby Jones, Walter Hagen, Francis Ouimet, Gene Sarazen, Alex Smith, MacDonald Smith, Glenna Collett, Virginia Van Wie, and Betty Hicks. Kennesaw Mountain Landis was a regular as were writers Grantland Rice and Rex Beach.

Left: In the late 1920s, the Belleview Biltmore circulated a brochure entitled When Winter Comes, hailing the area as "The Golfer's Southern Paradise." The cover showed an airplane flying in and a train arriving at the Belleview Biltmore proving its accessibility. Bellmen brought guests' luggage on handcars via tracks under the hotel then whisked the bags to the rooms by means of the steep, hidden staircases and freight elevators the help was required to use. During the 1920s, a single room rented for $4 although suites cost more and, of course, expenses were higher if the guest brought a retinue of servants. (Photo from the Belleview Mido Collection)

Below: Philip Manwaring Plant, born in 1901, was Maisie Cadwell Plant's only son and was adopted by Morton Plant. He lived the flamboyant life of a wealthy playboy, marrying three times before his death at the age of forty from pneumonia while exploring for the Smithsonian Institution. (Photo courtesy of the Henry B. Plant Museum Archives, Tampa, Florida)

Facing page: Philip Plant married his first wife, movie star and Broadway actress Constance Bennett (above) in 1925 when he was twenty-four. They lived in Beach Park in Tampa for a short time and divorced in 1929. Philip married Edna Dunham in 1934 and Marjorie King in 1938. He died in 1941. (Photo courtesy of the Henry B. Plant Museum Archives, Tampa, Florida)

Evenings found high rollers such as movie star Tyrone Power next door at Coe's Casino, a two-story, Spanish-style establishment with a dining room that could accommodate 150 and games of chance on the second floor. The law turned a blind eye with the understanding that the casino was strictly off limits to the locals. In the meantime, each winter season was a more spectacular success than the one previous—the Belleview's calendars and corridors were crammed with brilliant parties, famous guests and the money spilled like vintage wine. What could ever go wrong?

As the 1920s drew to a close, the Florida real estate market was already suffering from the adverse publicity created in the wake of several killer hurricanes and the inevitable reversal of stock prices that adjusted downward the artificially inflated property values. Then the final blow—Black Friday in October of 1929 when the stock market plummeted.

January of 1930 heralded one of the saddest, most subdued seasons in the Belleview Biltmore's thirty-three years. Familiar names and faces were

Above: From the time Henry B. Plant II was a small baby, his grandfather, Henry B. Plant, dreamed that one day Henry would take over the Plant Hotels which included the Tampa Bay Hotel, the Kissimmee Hotel, Ocala House, The Seminole in Winter Park, and the Fort Myers Hotel, but that was not to be. Following Morton's death in 1918, the hotel was sold to John McEntee Bowman of the Biltmore chain. Henry B. Plant II died in 1938 having sired two daughters, but no sons (see genealogical chart in Chapter I) so the Plant name was not directly carried on. (Photo courtesy of the Henry B. Plant Museum Archives, Tampa, Florida)

Left: The Bayou was one of the cottages built by wealthy families on the grounds as winter residences. According to the agreement, after five years the cottages became the property of the hotel. The eighty-year-old property is shown here a few days before it was demolished in 1992. (Photo by Laurie Counts)

Above: Brightwater *and* Magnolia *were also built by families on the hotel's property between 1920 and 1925. The Jacob Disston family, wealthy tool manufacturers from Philadelphia, built* Brightwater, *a sixteen-room "cottage." (Photo from the Ullman Collection)*

Above right: Sunset Cottage, *built in 1894–1895, now houses the hotel's accounting staff. (Photo from the Ullman Collection)*

Top of page: East Gate Cottage *was built before the construction of the Belleview Hotel. One of the few cottages left,* East Gate *is of Queen Anne Victorian architecture. Its intricate millwork and delightful tower still charm guests as they drive onto the Belleview Mido property. (Photo from the Ullman Collection)*

Left: Casa Mia, built in 1928 for drugstore magnate Charles A. Whelan, was occupied by the family until 1941. His guests included golfing great Arnold Palmer, Charles Comiskey of Chicago's Comiskey Park fame, and the Hoyts, manufacturers of Carter's Little Liver Pills. TV personality Fred Rogers, star of "Mr. Rogers' Neighborhood," lived in Casa Mia as a boy. (Photo from the Ullman Collection)

Above: Terrace Cottage built between 1903 and 1907 was demolished in 1992. Although lived in, it had fallen into an irreparable state of disrepair. (Photo by Laurie Counts)

Right: Rex Beach, best selling novelist and avid golfer, often wintered at the Belleview Biltmore and was frequently found on the fairways of the Belleview Biltmore courses. In 1948, Beach sold film rights to "Woman in Ambush" for $100,000, the highest price ever paid at that time for an unpublished manuscript. Movies from his novels included The Spoilers *and* World in His Arms *which starred Gregory Peck. At one time, he was president of the Belleview Biltmore Country Club. (Photo courtesy of Florida State Archives)*

By the 1920s when this photo was taken, and made into a postcard, the grounds of the Belleview Biltmore had flourished and matured. (Photo from the Belleview Mido Collection)

missing. And those guests who did come down for the winter were no longer so carefree. The daily trips to the office where the ticker tape was kept were no longer nonchalant, casual opportunities to chat. The brows of the beautiful people that winter were lined with worry, their jaws tight with apprehension.

And now the bills came due for the million-dollar expansion. And Bowman was broke. In fact, he even owed millions of dollars in back dividends to the stockholders. Triggered by Bowman's unexpected death on October 28, 1931, and the stock market crash, the Biltmore Hotel chain collapsed and each hotel, including the Belleview Biltmore, reverted to the stock and bondholders. In the Belleview Biltmore's case, many stockholders were from the area. The hotel remained open, leased by the receiver to a series of different resort operators until 1939 when it was purchased by Arnold Kirkeby.

Kirkeby, born June 12, 1901, in Chicago, Illinois, had started his business career as an investment security salesman in 1919. He'd made such a success of the first career that he'd moved on to become president of the K Corporation, the K Natus Corporation, Warwick Realty and formed the Kirkeby Hotel chain. Kirkeby, who died March 1, 1962, in Los Angeles where he is buried in Forest Lawn, ultimately moved his business interests to California where he was a director of the City National Bank in Beverly Hills and the Magnavox Corporation.

Kirkeby was, in fact, the owner in March 1941 when an era ended. That month Daniel Willard, president of the Baltimore and Ohio Railroad,

This aerial photograph gives a bird's-eye view of the palm-lined road as it curved its way to the hotel's entrance. (Photo courtesy of the Town of Belleair)

Above: The Belleview Biltmore traditionally opened its season with an impressive flag ceremony held at noon the first week in January. A color guard, such as the guard from the Turner-Brandon American Legion Post 7, raised the colors on the flagpole near the first tees of the two golf courses. Hundreds of local people and guests witnessed the ceremony each year. (Photo from the Belleview Mido Collection)

Right: Federal Judge Kennesaw M. Landis, was one of the country's most revered, respected men until his death in 1944. Landis was named first baseball commissioner in 1921 after a scandal in 1919 when eight members of the Chicago White Sox accepted a bribe to throw the World Series to the Cincinnati Reds. He took quick, firm action to restore the confidence of the fans in the sport. Shown here second from the left, he wintered at the Belleview Biltmore for nearly twenty years, often playing golf with his friends on the hotel golf courses. (Photo from the Belleview Mido Collection)

became the last railroad president to travel to the Belleview Biltmore by private rail car.

Despite the uncertain economic times, Kirkeby and his wife, known as "the most gracious host from coast to coast," reportedly had three successful seasons even hosting the Brooklyn Dodgers for spring training of 1940. Then World War II erupted in the wake of Japan's bombing of Pearl Harbor. The aftershock of that attack rocked the entire country and launched the Belleview Biltmore into one of the most unusual chapters of its already intriguing history when its "guests" became servicemen in the U.S. Army Air Corps.

The Belleview Biltmore was completely self-sufficient with its own post office, police and fire departments that also served the Town of Belleair, with the general manager acting as postmaster. In 1942 the three departments were moved off hotel property and became the responsibility of the Town of Belleair. The hotel also had its own power plant and water pump system until the government required them to hook up to Florida Power in 1943.

By 1942, concerns about money, stocks, options, and futures had been supplanted by the overwhelming wave of outrage and patriotism that engulfed the nation. Everyone was involved in World War II whether it was growing a Victory garden, selling or buying War Bonds or coping with rationing. The Belleview Biltmore entered the war effort when it was requisitioned by the U.S. Army Air Corps to provide extra housing for servicemen training at MacDill and Drew Air Fields in Tampa.

Immediately the hotel's ledgers and registers, antique furniture, furnishings, supplies and equipment were removed and stored in warehouses. Later these items were used in other Kirkeby hotels or sold at auction resulting in the loss of a major portion of the hotel's history. By summer, the airmen had moved in. The hotel's seventeen hundred windows as well as the glorious panels between the hallway and the Tiffany Room were slathered with heavy coats

Above: John McEntee Bowman was one of this country's most successful hotel chain owners and operators. Born July 20, 1875, in Toronto, Canada, Bowman was assistant to Gustav Baumann when Baumann founded the Biltmore chain. Baumann promoted him to vice president, then he was named president when Baumann died in an accident. Bowman organized a company and took over the Hotel Manhattan, then the Ansonia. In 1917, he bought the Murray Hill and Belmont Hotels, then the Commodore. Bowman made his entry into Florida hostelries with the purchase in 1919 of the Belleview, adding the Biltmore name. At the same time, he purchased the Belleview's sister hotel, the Griswold in New London, Connecticut. In this photo taken circa 1920, Bowman (far right) and associates (from left) Charles Flynn, George E. Merrick, creator of Coral Gables, and Roy Jackson were scouting a site at Coco Plum Beach on the East Coast of Florida. In 1926, Bowman in partnership with Merrick opened the Miami Biltmore. (Photo courtesy of the South Florida Historical Museum, Miami, Florida)

Above: Taken in January 1930 on the Belleview Biltmore golf course with the hotel in the background, this photo is of a very famous foursome. From left: Rube Marzard, played for Boston Braves, New York Giants, and Brooklyn Dodgers, Gene Sarazen, U.S. Open 1922, 1932, PGA 1922, 1923, 1933, British Open 1932, Masters 1935, PGA Hall of Fame 1940, World Hall of Fame 1974; Babe Ruth, pitcher then outfielder for the Boston Red Sox and New York Yankees player; Johnny Farrell, 1927 U.S. Open, PGA golf professional. (Photo courtesy of Howard Noe)

of black paint to block escaping light. The stained-glass ceiling was not painted black. Submarine scares were common as nervous soldiers and Floridians kept watch on the waters of Clearwater Bay and the Gulf of Mexico beyond.

For more than a year, the Belleview Biltmore's grounds resonated with the pounding of feet marching in unison, with the cadence of snare drums and bugle calls, with the slangy jive talk of America's GIs who spoke of zoot suits and danced the jitterbug. These warriors-in-training were a far cry from the Belleview's normal roster of refined and elegant guests.

Above: This natural hazard on the east course was so challenging, it resulted in the fourteenth hole being described by Life magazine as one of the "Eighteen Great Golf Holes in America." (Photo from the Belleview Mido Collection)

Left: The west lounge, a sunny room with a spectacular view from its wall of windows and comfortable wicker furniture, was a perfect place to spend an afternoon relaxing with a friend or a book. (Photo from the Belleview Mido Collection)

Top of page: Sun worshippers gathered around the flag in front of the Belleview Biltmore Cabana Club. Added by Arnold Kirkeby for the 1941 winter season, guests enjoyed it until the winter season of 1963 when the new Cabana Club was built. (Photo from the Belleview Mido Collection)

Above: The year was 1940, the time was the cocktail hour and these hotel guests swapped golf stories and reviewed the day. From left: Mrs. Byrne Bower, Mrs. Charles White, Mrs. Richard Ware, Mrs. Beber McFarland, Capt. Richard Ware, and Mr. Byrne Bower. (Photo from the Belleview Mido Collection)

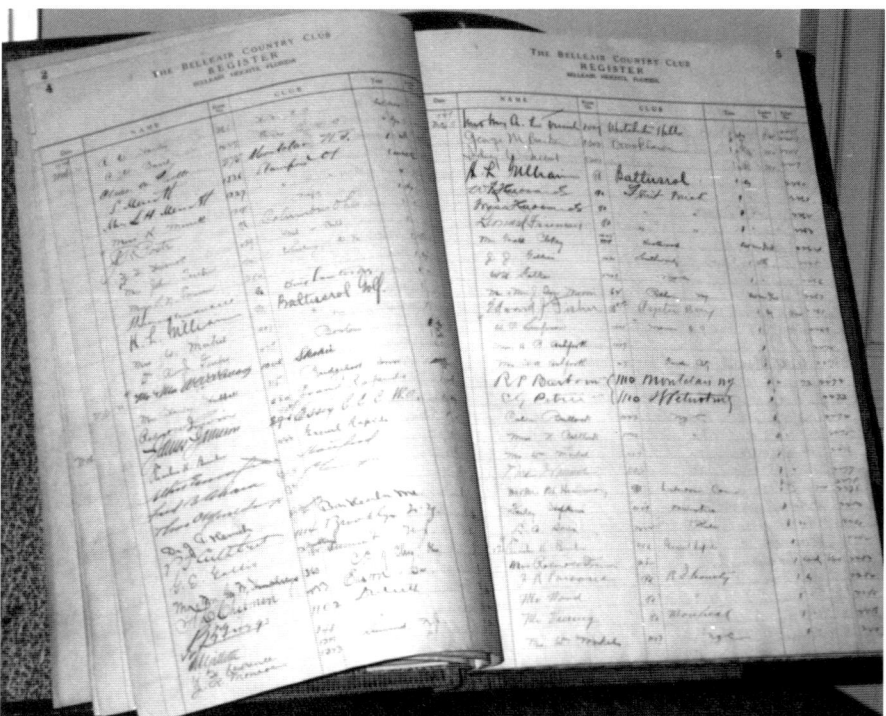

Above: The hotel country club's handwritten registers were a virtual who's who of noteworthy and famous names. Unfortunately, during World War II when the U.S. Army Air Corps moved into the hotel, most of the hotel's records were lost and never recovered. (Photo by Esther B. Colcord)

By August of 1943, the U.S. Army Corps had moved out and the Queen's corridors were silent for the first time.

During its tenancy, the military had been extremely concerned about the possibility of a fire. Ironically, the last day the Air Corps was in residence, the installation of a brand-new, state-of-the-art $100,000 sprinkler system was completed. In 1944, Kirkeby sold the Belleview Biltmore to Ed C. Wright at auction for $275,000. Wright, a wealthy real estate investor living in St. Petersburg, Florida, was born December 30, 1891, in St. Mary's, Georgia. He moved to St. Petersburg in 1907 to go to high school. A multimillionaire, Ed C. Wright made his fortune during the Depression dealing in municipal bonds and defaulted coupons. During Wright's ownership, the Belleview Biltmore remained closed, but her doors would soon reopen.

Left: Having survived the decades, the ninety-six leaded glass panes created in the style of Louis Comfort Tiffany still span the ceiling of the Tiffany Room. Enlarged in the early 1920s, the Tiffany Room seats eight hundred. While occupied by the U.S. Army Air Corps during World War II, fear of enemy submarines in the Gulf waters prompted the servicemen to paint the windows—but not the Tiffany-style panes—black to prevent the hotel from being seen at night. The chandeliers were covered with seven coats of olive green paint. When stripped after the war, the chandeliers were found to be solid brass. (Photo from the Belleview Mido Collection)

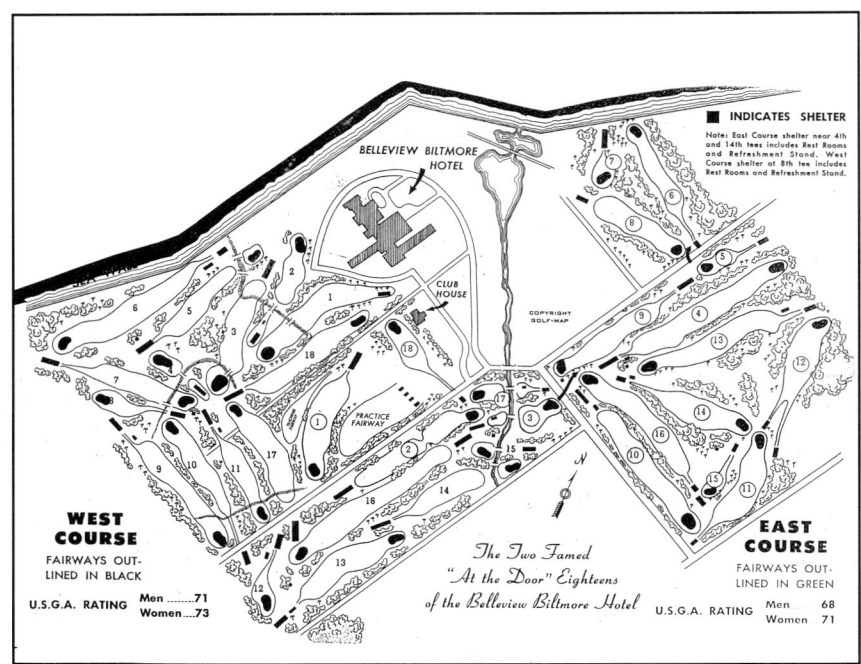

Above: Schematic drawings of the famed east and west golf courses. (From the Belleview Mido Archives)

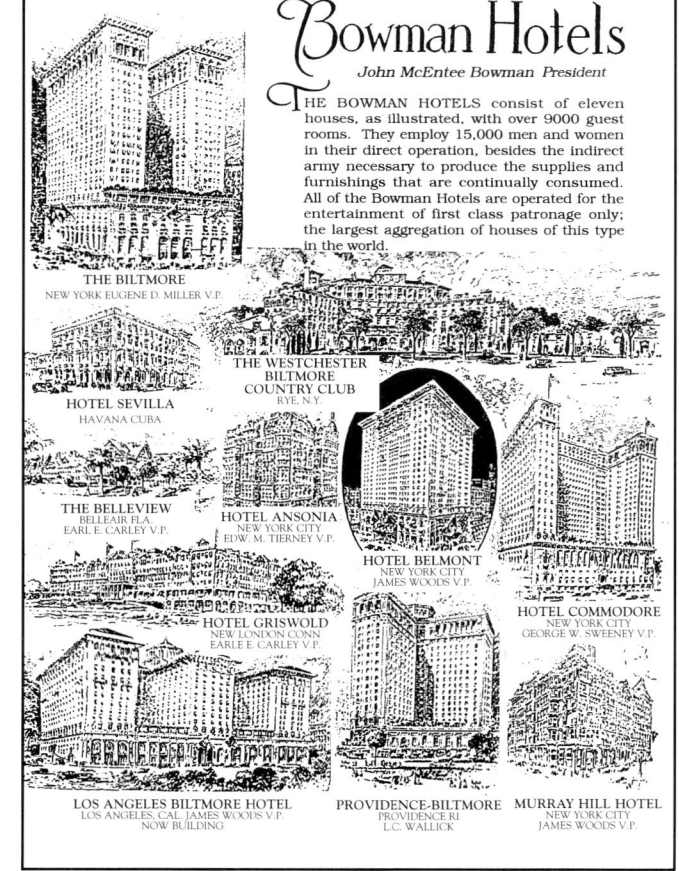

Left: Brochure from Bowman Hotels showing the roster of hotels owned and operated by Bowman during the chain's heyday. (Photo from the Belleview Mido Collection)

Above: This tea garden postcard dated 1929 depicts a pleasant place where ladies enjoyed their afternoons while waiting for their husbands to come off the golf course. (Photo from the Belleview Mido Collection)

Right: Built in 1897 with more than 150 rooms and east of the of main hotel, the dormitory was constructed of heart of pine lumber to house hotel employees during the four-month season. It consisted of three full floors and two additional floors built into the roof space. (Photo from the Ullman Collection)

Left: Pergola and Tea House—lovely gardens and a pleasant shelter from the blazing Florida sun. (Photo from the Belleview Mido Collection)

Above: Ring Lardner, sportswriter for papers in St. Louis, Chicago, and Boston, was also a prolific writer of baseball short stories. Even while wintering at the Belleview Biltmore where he thoroughly enjoyed the golf courses, he worked steadily, writing short stories such as One Hit, One Error, One Left. *These manuscripts were sent from Clearwater, published in the* Saturday Evening Post *and later in his book* Ring Around the Bases. *(Photo from the Belleview Mido Collection)*

Left: Another famous golfer, movie/radio personality and writer who wintered at the Belleview Biltmore was Grantland Rice. From 1933 to 1943, he had a program on football. From 1920 until 1936, he was editor of The American Golfer *and also author of two books on golf—which was his favorite game despite his expertise in other sports. Best known for his syndicated column called "The Sportlight," Rice immortalized the Notre Dame backfield in 1924 when he dubbed them "The Four Horsemen." (Photo courtesy of Special Collections, Heard Library, Vanderbilt University)*

Above: In this photo taken circa 1920, a horse-drawn carriage moved to the right to let the vehicle pass on the entrance bridge to the Hotel. It was not uncommon to see horseback riders, even women in long skirts riding sidesaddle, cross this little bridge on their way to the Belleview Biltmore Hotel. Speed limit for automobiles was twelve miles per hour. (Photo from the Ullman Collection)

Left: The pool house, in the 1930s, was a popular spot for swimming. The upper deck was removed in 1940 when sunbathing became a popular pastime. The pool contained an impressive 200,000 gallons of water which were constantly chlorinated and filtered and maintained at seventy-two degrees. (Photo from the Belleview Mido Collection)

Top of page: Dubbed Coe's Casino after William Coe, the man who built it, this two-story Spanish-style casino was absolutely off limits to local people, but VIP guests including the Duke of Windsor, auto magnate James Studebaker, movie star Tyrone Power, and Meyer Guggenheim were chauffeured to the Casino in Belleview Biltmore limousines. After Coe's death, the casino was sold. In 1949, the new owners had a run-in with the law and closed the casino. Years later, the building was reopened as Trinity College for Seminary students. Evangelist Billy Graham attended Trinity. (Photo from the Belleview Mido Collection)

Above: At this dock photographed in the 1930s, you could board a boat for Sand Key and the Cabana Club, go fishing, take a sightseeing cruise or watch the fishermen bring in the day's catch as this man is doing. (Photo from the Ullman Collection)

Above: The U.S. Air Force 672nd Unit Band played at the service club and other military functions at the Belleview Biltmore Hotel during the hotel's stint as a military barracks in World War II. (Photo from the Belleview Mido Collection)

Left: This brochure from the 1920s was entitled "Belleair—An Idea Winter Playground." (Brochure from the Belleview Mido Archives)

Left: Ed C. Wright, a quiet, publicity-shy man, became a huge landowner during the Depression and World War II by buying acreage and properties at discounted prices including the Belleview Biltmore. At one time, Wright owned ten square miles of property in Pinellas County and his annual tax bills weighed forty-two pounds. (Courtesy of St. Petersburg Times)

Right: While training at MacDill Air Force Base testing B25s, J. R. Richards was billeted at the Belleview Biltmore. Richards posed on the south lawn where the tennis courts had been in more peaceful times. (Photo courtesy of Mr. J. R. Richards)

Facing page, far left: By October 1942, the Belleview Biltmore had settled into her new role as a military barracks housing three thousand airmen twelve to a room. A tent city was erected on the grounds to shelter the overflow. The practice range, first and eighteenth fairways of the west golf course were used as drill fields. While stationed at the Belleview Biltmore, twenty-one-year-old Burner C. Stewart had his picture taken on the steps of one of the hotel cottages. Like many other service men, Stewart revisited the hotel and, in 1994, donated this photo to the hotel's archives. (Photo Courtesy of Mr. and Mrs. Burner C. Stewart)

Facing page, left: Company bugler Harry J. Wilson, a private from Dayton, Ohio, earned a special place in the memories of the soldiers he was stationed with at the Belleview Biltmore in 1943. One of his duties was playing reveille to awaken the troops at 5:00 a.m. One morning as he stood at the foot of the grand stairway and played reveille, he was deluged by an avalanche of boots and shoes. It was 4:00 a.m. not 5:00 and the servicemen had not returned from maneuvers until after midnight. (Photo courtesy of Mr. and Mrs. Harry Wilson)

Golf foursomes were common on the courses at the Belleview. This one, however, was special for it included royalty. From left: Belleview golf pro Tommy Harmon, Belleview manager Donald Church, the Duke of Windsor, and owner Bernard F. Powell. The Duke enjoyed the weather, the golf, and mingled both with other guests and the staff. The suite he occupied is now used as an office by Powell who sold the hotel in 1990. A brass plate on the door identifies it as the Duke of Windsor Suite. (Photo from the Belleview Mido Collection)

CHAPTER

THREE
1946–1972

In 1946, Wright sold the beautiful if somewhat bedraggled "White Queen of the Gulf" to a group of investors from Detroit headed by Bernard and Mary Powell, his sister Nora Peabody, and Roger L. Stevens. Mr. Powell was an attorney admitted to practice before the U.S. Supreme Court. Mr. Stevens was a part owner in the Empire State Building in New York City and a Broadway theatrical producer. He was also the guiding light behind the Kennedy Performing Arts Center in Washington, D.C.

The new owners faced an awesome challenge. The hotel had received no maintenance for four years. The exterior needed a good coat of paint. The Belleview Biltmore's pride, her golf courses, were knee high in weeds, grass, and palmettoes. The grounds were overgrown. The rooms were mere shells.

In the wake of World War II, shortages were a way of life and the new owners had to procure beds, bureaus, tables, lamps, bed linens, blankets, and draperies for nearly four hundred guest rooms and two hundred rooms in the employees' quarters.

In the kitchens, only the boilers and some stoves (still used in the main kitchen) remained so it was also necessary to locate pots, pans, china, silverware, glassware to serve six hundred guests as well as four hundred workers.

Somehow the impossible was accomplished and the Belleview Biltmore was renovated and redecorated in time for a gala reopening on January 10, 1947.

The years ahead were devoted to restoring the Queen to her original splendor. "For 10 years," manager Don Church told a reporter from the

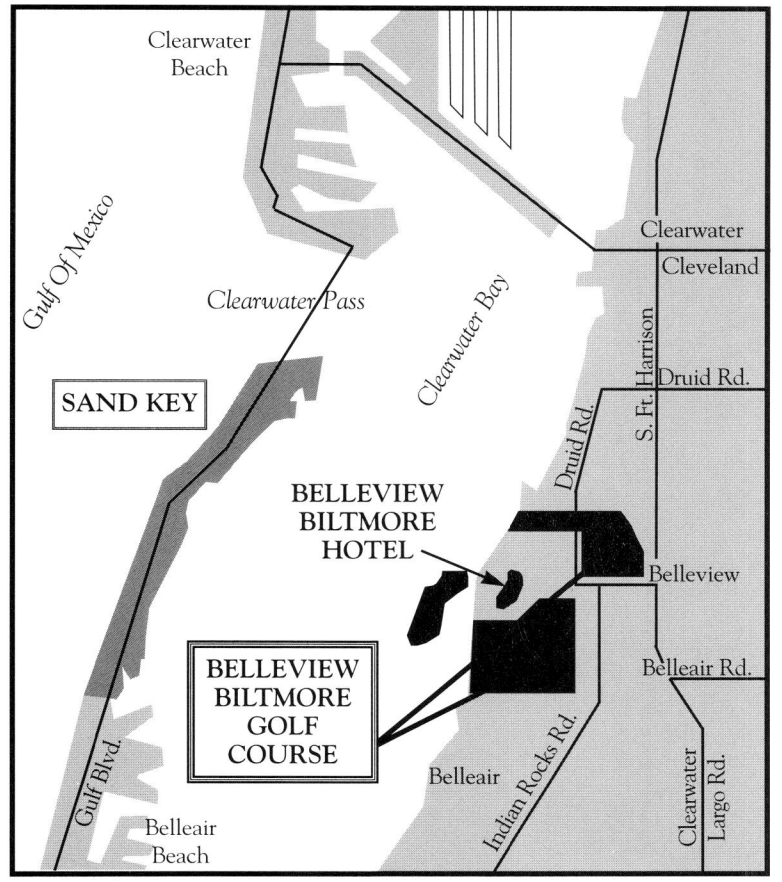

Facing page: Cal Gilford, popular band leader and music director, appeared at the Belleview Biltmore for eight seasons in the late 1940s and early 1950s. The band played at the swimming pool every day for lunch, always opening the set with "Anchors Aweigh." The band also played in the lounge before dinner and provided dance music for the rest of the evening as well as for shows in the Starlight Room. After leaving the Belleview Biltmore, the Cal Gilford orchestra played opposite the combined Dorsey band at the Statler Hotel in New York. (Photo courtesy of the Cal Gilford family)

Left: This map published in the St. Petersburg Times in August of 1969 depicted the location of the Belleview Biltmore in relation to Clearwater Beach as well as the Belleview Biltmore's famous golf courses.

Below: The Starlight Room was, and is, a popular place for parties and celebrations. Shown here, Cal Gilford and his orchestra were setting up for a Saint Patrick's Day dance. (Photo from the Belleview Mido Collection)

Belleair Breeze

VOLUME 12, NUMBER 3   OCTOBER, 1971   BELLEAIR, FLORIDA

GREEK DANCERS TO ENTERTAIN AT ANNUAL MEETING OF PROPERTY OWNERS ASS'N.

On Thursday, October 28, at 8 p.m. in the Civic Center, the Belleair Civic & Property Owners will have its annual meeting. The highlight of the evening will be a performance by a group of children from Tarpon Springs who will perform traditional Greek dances in costume.

Following a brief review of the year's activities by the President there will be the annual election of officers and directors and such other business as may come before the meeting. **Mayor Fred Wilder** and Town Manager **John Coleman** will give brief reports, followed by refreshments.

All members are urged to attend what promises to be an informative and entertaining evening.

GROUND BROKEN FOR FIRST U. S. STEEL CONDOMINIUM

Ground was broken Sept. 9 for the first eight-story condominium that U.S. Steel Realty Development Division will build on the bayfront near the Belleview Biltmore Hotel.

The first building will offer 96 units and is the first of three planned in the Bayshore series. At the time of the groundbreaking, almost one third of the units were already reserved, company officials said.

All units in this series feature two large bedrooms and two baths, living-dining areas and wide balconies with a commanding view of Clearwater Bay. Prices will range from $40,900 to $53,400.

Other condominiums planned will be as large as three bedrooms with prices ranging upward to $100,000.

Joseph Dembeck, president of USS Realty Development Corporation said that "we came, not to exploit the community, but to share in its growth in such a way as to preserve and enhance those features which have given it its own unique appeal."

RAINY DAY CEREMONY—Joseph Dembeck, president of U.S. Steel Realty Development Corporation, with an assist from two-year-old Lisa Lizak, niece of a project secretary, turned the first spadeful of soggy earth in the rain, marking the beginning of construction on the Bayshore series of condominiums planned for construction near the Belleview Biltmore Hotel.

Working under an umbrella because of a drizzling rain, Joseph Dembeck, president of U.S. Steel Realty Development Corporation turned the first spade of sod for an eight-story condominium on September 9, 1969. He was assisted by two-year old Lisa Lizak, niece of a project secretary. The story, which made the front page of this issue of the Belleair Breeze, *reported this was the first of three ninety-six-unit buildings to be built on the bayfront side of the Belleview Biltmore Hotel. (Photo from the Town of Belleair Archives)*

St. Petersburg Times, "we replaced plaster and carpeting ruined by rain through windows left open." In 1948, new plumbing and wiring was also installed. The renovation was from the inside out.

The west course was opened for the 1947 season; eleven holes of the east course were opened in 1949, but it wasn't until the 1957 season that both courses were once again open. In 1958, the Belleair Fire Department which had been housed on the grounds since 1917 was relocated in town. The "White Queen of the Gulf" settled back into her role as a winter resort for the wealthy, but change was again on the horizon. In 1969, several events took place which directly impacted the Belleview Biltmore. Real estate magnate Ed C. Wright died February 1; in August, his heirs sold 157 acres on Sand Key and 290 acres in Belleair to U.S. Steel for $10 million. The Belleair site included the two Belleview Biltmore golf courses. The area was on the brink of the wave of massive, unrelenting growth that would inundate Southwest Florida in the decades ahead.

Above: During his stay at the Belleview Biltmore in the 1953 winter season, the Duke of Windsor (center right) even acted as judge of the costume contest at a masked ball. (Photo courtesy of Donna Fox)

Left: These five-globed lampposts lend a romantic glow to the grounds illuminating the curved entrance drive to the hotel, a salute to the Belleview Biltmore's Victorian heritage. (Brochure from the Belleview Mido Archives)

The huge cornucopias sculpted from ice appeared to pour tempting tropical fruits. The kitchen staff posed behind this festive and tasty array of pastries that dominated the dessert table which was probably prepared for one of the Belleview Biltmore's famous Sunday brunches. In a 3 1/2-month season in the late 1970s when this photo was taken, Church estimated that the staff of thirty cooks used 32,500 pounds of poultry, 55,000 pounds or more than 27 1/2 tons of beef, 6,225 pounds of coffee, 20,650 dozens of fresh eggs, and 15,000 pounds of butter. (Photo from the Belleview Mido Collection)

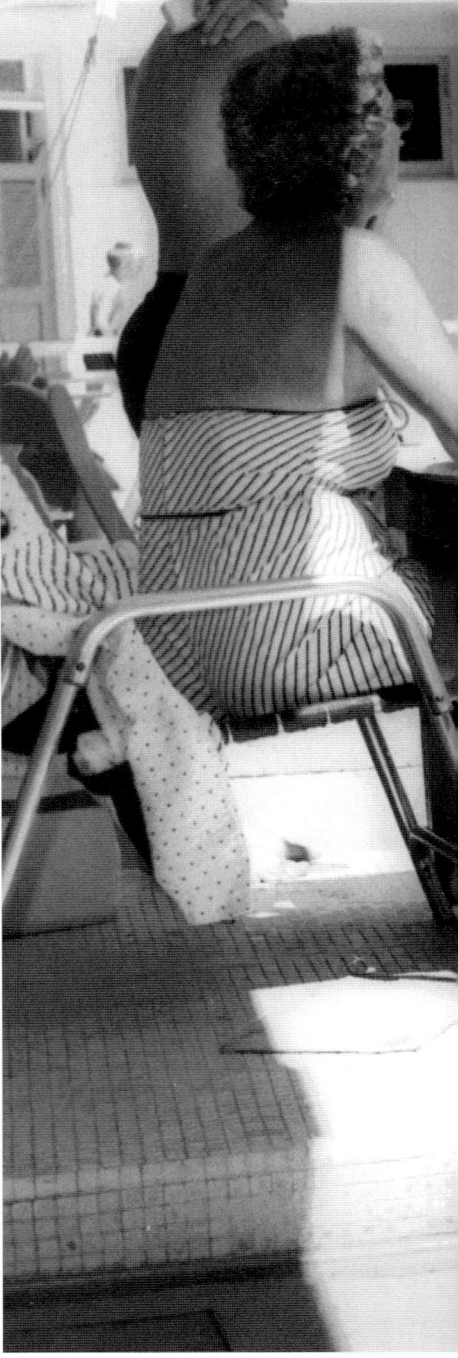

Left: The administrative staff of the Belleview Biltmore posed on the steps for this photo in the early 1970s. In the front row from left: Donald Church, manager from 1948 through 1973, and owners Bernard Powell and Nora Peabody. (Photo from the Belleview Mido Collection)

The pool was enjoyed by the children who wintered at the hotel with their parents. One of Kathy Powell Strong's favorite memories concerns pool director Scotty McAlpin. A small, wiry man with a thick Scottish brogue, McAlpin marked the children's heights on the wall of the poolhouse. Each year, he repeated the process to show them how much they had grown. When the pool area had to be painted, he carefully copied the measurements on a separate sheet of paper and recopied them on the wall when the painters finished. Strong, daughter of owner Bernie Powell, lived at the hotel in the winter. She remembers sitting on the edge of the pool for one hour after eating. Anyone who jumped in a minute too soon was banned from the pool the rest of the day. Strict as he was, the children loved Scotty. (Photo from the Belleview Mido Collection)

Left: Former guest Marion Grimm donated this postcard to the hotel museum. Dated 1955, her message read, "Friends of ours are 'conventioning' at this place for a week and love it all. . . ." Weather was perfect the entire week of their stay and golfing, swimming was ideal for the recreation between seasons. (Photo from the Belleview Mido Archives)

Below: Kathy Powell Strong also has delightful memories of growing up at the Belleview Biltmore, of playing in the hidden staircases and attending the little red schoolhouse, of tree forts, hotel-arranged swimming meets and pool parties, and making fishing poles from bamboo. "It was a wonderful place to grow up," she says today. (Photo by Esther B. Colcord)

Above: Lucy Disston Gilpin, daughter of the late Jacob Disston, is shown here in 1978 with museum director Ralph Reed during a visit to the Pinellas County Historical Museum. As a child, Mrs. Gilpin spent many winters in Brightwater, a cottage her family built on the Belleview Biltmore grounds. The cottage designs had to be approved by the Plant family and title reverted to hotel ownership after five years. From then on, families had to pay substantial rents to stay in the cottages they had erected. (Photo from the Belleview Mido Collection)

Two happy tennis enthusiasts left the Tennis Shop ready for a smashing game on the courts. Lessons by Tennis Pro Michael Gaylorde were free to guests, but cost outsiders a staggering $4 an hour. (Photo from the Belleview Mido Collection)

Facing page, above: In the 1950s when this photo was taken, the children's private dining room was still used for that purpose. Built originally so that the children and their nannies could dine comfortably and yet be out of the public eye, the room today is used for board meetings. (Photo from the Belleview Mido Collection)

Facing page, below: Mrs. William Webster and Belleview Biltmore Tennis Pro Michael Gaylorde paused to pose behind the net of the Har-Tru court. (Photo from the Belleview Mido Collection)

Above: The first tee was positioned so close, golf was within easy walking distance. In this photo from the 1950s, interested guests and fellow golfers watched as a golfer took that "first swing." (Photo from the Belleview Mido Collection)

This aerial photo reveals how vast the Belleview Biltmore/Mido and its grounds are. The Belleview green roof covers 2 1/2 acres. (Photo from the Belleview Mido Collection)

Above: It was a good day on The Gremlin, *the Belleview Biltmore's launch, as evidenced by the smiles of these happy fishermen. They were perhaps thinking about getting the Belleview Biltmore chef to cook their "catch of the day." (Photo from the Belleview Mido Collection)*

Right: Edward Everett Horton (right), star of stage, screen, and television, was another of the Belleview Biltmore's noted guests. Here, he enjoyed an evening in the Starlight Room. After a movie career in which he played the sidekick or butler in the Fred Astaire–Ginger Rogers movies, Horton played recurring roles in the television series "F Troop" and "The Cara Williams Show." He died of cancer in September of 1970. (Photo from the Belleview Mido Collection)

Above: Kathy Powell Strong recalls "the wonderful boat captain, Captain Alexander," who took the gangs of school kids at the hotel "back and forth to the beach in the Cola, the hotel's private launch." (Photo from the Belleview Mido Collection)

Left: A cheery room with matching curtains and dust ruffle, it was typical of quarters provided in the Belleview Biltmore dormitory. The photo shows Donna Fox, a Belleview Biltmore waitress in 1953 relaxing in her room. Rules were strict. According to a former employee, it was lights out at 11:30 p.m. Doors were locked and workers who weren't in their rooms were in serious trouble. Shoes and fingernails were inspected daily and staff members were fined twenty-five cents if they weren't in the dining room for breakfast on time. (Photo courtesy of Donna Fox)

Below: By the time the brochure from which this page was taken was published in 1972, all traces of wartime had vanished. The ninety-six panes of Tiffany-style glass in the Tiffany Room (top) admitted the brilliant Florida sunshine and the guest rooms (bottom) had been completely refurnished and refurbished. (Photo from the Belleview Mido Collection)

Right: As children were encouraged to become more and more visible, the Belleview Biltmore staff enthusiastically responded, planning even more activities for their youthful guests. An Easter Egg Hunt on the lawn with a personal visit from the Easter Bunny became an annual event. (Photo from the Belleview Mido Collection)

Above: Flag raising ceremonies were traditionally held at high noon on the opening day of each season in mid-January. A color guard, often from the Turner-Brandon American Legion Post 7, officiated. The season closed in April. Times changed, the wealthy people who had wintered at the Belleview Biltmore for decades passed on and the hotel's marketing strategy had to change. In the winter of 1986, the Belleview Biltmore began staying open year round. (Photo from the Belleview Mido Collection)

Above: Ed C. Wright's purchase of the Belleview Biltmore properties did not include the Cabana Club on Sand Key which was sold to Charles Thacher who leased it to the Belleview Biltmore. In 1963, Powell built and equipped the Cabana and Beach Club incorporating many suggestions from guests. It now provided not only a beautiful white sandy, gently sloping beach across the Intracoastal Waterway from the hotel, but attractive cabanas, dressing rooms, and a complete kitchen and bar. Transportation by boat or van was provided by the hotel. In the summers, when the hotel was closed, the facility was operated as a club for local guests. It was a popular place for weddings, wedding receptions, banquets, and meetings. (Photo from the Belleview Mido Collection)

Above: Shuffleboard, always popular with guests, was a good way to combine moderate exercise with friendly competition while everyone enjoyed Florida's mild winter weather. It was also another of the many activities the Belleview Biltmore offered guests. (Photo from the Belleview Mido Collection)

Right: In the 1920s, the Candlelight Room was used by the ladies for afternoon coffee and tea and was "off limits" to gentlemen. That changed and in 1950 a bar complete with a trap door in the floor was installed. The stairs leading down from the trapdoor connected with the underground tracks where deliveries were brought by handcars. Supplies could be restocked out of the view of the guests. It is now a small dining room and adjoining lounge. (Photo from the Belleview Mido Collection)

Left: This postcard depicts the little red schoolhouse where children of the guests who wintered at the Belleview Biltmore attended class. Retired schoolteacher Mrs. Peebles, shown here on the porch, recruited other retired teachers from Clearwater. The children brought their textbooks from the northern schools to study. Mrs. Peebles and her staff conducted lessons from nine until twelve. Usually, when the children returned north they were ahead of their classmates because they received virtually individual tutoring. (Photo from the Belleview Mido Collection)

Below: The scattering of bright striped wooden balls about the lawn was a sure sign that a brisk game of croquet was in progress. (Photo from the Belleview Mido Collection)

Above: This "head on" photo of the old movie projector details the specifications of the Peerless Magnarc which is now on display in the Belleview Mido museum. (Photo from the Esther B. Colcord)

Above: Assistant Projectionist Dave Franke remembers lighting the 100,000 candlepower wick which projected the image on the screen. Wicks lasted roughly 6 1/2 hours and took seven minutes to change. Movies were shown Tuesday and Thursday nights in the Starlight Room. The projectionist entered through the basement and slipped up the back stairs. "You just stayed out of sight of the guests and did your job," said Dave. Security clearance was a must. (Photo by Esther B. Colcord)

A number of prestigious corporations and organizations held their meetings at the Belleview Biltmore. General Electric, for example, during a twenty-year period, held eighteen conferences at the Belleview Biltmore for its vice presidents and general managers. U.S. Steel held its annual meetings there for several years. One of the most significant in the world of sports was the U.S. Lawn Tennis Association. In 1968, that meeting was held at the Belleview Biltmore. Shown here behind the coveted Davis Cup was Donald Church, Belleview manager, flanking R. T. Kelleher of Beverly Hills, 1968 president of the USLTA. On the right was owner Powell. (Photo from the Belleview Mido Collection)

This staff of cooks was the behind-the-scenes crew responsible for the three thousand meals served daily to guests, visitors, and employees during the height of the season. (Photo from the Belleview Mido Collection)

Known in the 1990s as St. Andrews Pub and located in the basement, it was known as the Bimini Room when this photo was taken. Notice the shells and coral used as decorating accessories on the partitions on the right and on wall shelves to the left. (Photo from the Belleview Mido Collection)

This undated aerial probably taken in the late 1970s or early 1980s shows the Belleview Biltmore center left, Clearwater Bay and Sand Key upper left, the Beach and Cabana Club in Clearwater Bay north of the hotel, the condominiums built by U.S. Steel between the hotel and the Cabana Club and Sand Key upper left. (Photo from the Belleview Mido Collection)

CHAPTER

FOUR
1973–1997

The past quarter-century has seen change become the constant for the Belleview Biltmore. Although U.S. Steel had outbid Powell to purchase the golf courses, Powell negotiated a lease with U.S. Steel enabling the Belleview Biltmore's guests to use them. All golfers benefited from renovations U.S. Steel began that same year. Fairway watering systems were installed, greens and tees were enlarged and reshaped; several holes were lengthened and redesigned.

Powell next addressed the refurbishing of the Belleview Biltmore's exterior. Prior to 1974, the "Queen" kept three or four painters busy for up to six months every time she required repainting. When the cost of 1,000-plus gallons of paint was added to the labor expense, repainting became an expensive proposition. Powell decided to cover the hotel with aluminum siding. It would not alter the hotel's appearance and could reduce painting maintenance by 95 percent. Even the re-siding was a mammoth project because of the hotel's size; the Belleview Biltmore needed 1,800-plus squares of siding and more than 5.8 miles of aluminum window trim. A crew of fifteen men worked ten hours a day, six days a week for four months.

However, more than the hotel's exterior was changing. The hotel industry was reflecting a transformation in the nation's social structure. The old guard was dying and new fortunes were being made by younger, more restless people. The guests accustomed to spending an entire winter at the Belleview Biltmore were being replaced by people who would fly in to stay ten days to a maximum of three weeks.

The administrative staff responsible for the day-to-day operation of the Belleview Mido in 1996—Food and Beverage Director Paul Seastrom, Rooms Division Manager Kathleen Moore, General Manager Jeffry Martin, Controller Mike Meza, and Director of Sales and Marketing Oliver Kugler. (Photo from the Belleview Mido Collection)

Above: Another noted visitor in 1996 was Robert Gourdin (center), national sales manager of Moet Chandon. In this photo taken in St. Andrews Pub, he is talking to Belleview Mido Marketing Coordinator Karin Case and Belleview Mido Food and Beverage Director Paul Seastrom. (Photo from the Belleview Mido Collection)

Left: Patricia Counts, head tour guide, pauses on the grand staircase to orient the tour group. For five years, Counts and her assistant tour guides who are employed by the hotel have conducted tours seven days a week at 11:00 a.m. for guests and visitors. In the photo, Counts was dressed for a Victorian Christmas. (Photo courtesy of Patricia Counts)

Above: In 1996, Lady Margaret Thatcher, former British prime minister, was welcomed to the Belleview Mido by General Manager Jeffry Martin. (Photo from the Belleview Mido Collection)

Generating sufficient room turnover to replace income derived from seasonal guests was a challenge calling for different marketing strategies. The emphasis shifted to conventions and, while these soon accounted for 60 percent of the Belleview Biltmore's revenue, other problems surfaced. Wages had risen as had the cost of food and energy. And it was becoming tough to make money while staying open only 3 1/2 months each year.

Not all the news was bad by any means. In 1979, the Belleview Biltmore was named to the National Register of Historic Places and received a certificate now on display in the museum. In 1985, the Belleview Biltmore received two very prestigious designations: *Mobil Travel Guide* gave the Belleview Biltmore the Four-Star Award and *World Tennis Magazine* named her a Five-Star Tennis Resort.

In December of 1985 after nearly forty years, Powell and his co-owners signed a three-year lease-option agreement with a partnership comprised of developer Charles Rutenberg, spa executive Salu Devnani, and Belleview General Manager Christopher Reyelt. The partnership was to operate the Belleview Biltmore and one of their most important decisions was to keep her open year-round. The partnership also poured $10 million into a renovation of the guest rooms and the construction of a new, luxurious, state-of-the-art spa.

Then, in mid-1987, a serious problem arose. U.S. Steel, reacting to a down turn in the steel market, put the golf courses on the market. This time, despite Powell's efforts, the courses were purchased by the Belleair Country Club, a newly formed organization owned by its 980 members. As of June 1, 1987,

Facing page: A hundred years have passed, times and styles have changed and yet this new lobby with its infusion of light, both direct and reflected, pays homage to the Victorian age in which the Belleview Mido was constructed. While guests are enchanted by the aluminum chandelier overhead, the bronze statue of Themis, the Greek goddess of law and justice, reminds them of the hotel's heritage. (Photo from the Belleview Mido Collection)

Above: Once the purchase by the Mido Development Corporation was finalized, the construction of a new east entrance was planned as part of the first phase of a $10 million facelift. The new entrance was designed by architect Argie McElmurry to be more accessible to the handicapped and closer to parking. (Photo from the Belleview Mido Collection)

Far right: Beneath this grand hotel is a virtual maze of pathways. The sidewalls were originally brick, but paved with concrete during the Belleview Mido's renovation. Although the hotel now has new wiring and steel beams, exposed wiring using old ceramic spools called "tube and knob" is still in place. Plumbing pipes are visible, too, giving visitors taking the tour a fascinating view of the technology of the past. (Photo by Esther B. Colcord)

Right: The east basement contained narrow tracks for the handcars used to transport baggage from the incoming trains to the hotel. The east basement also contained hotel service areas and storage rooms. The west basement originally had a bowling alley, bicycle shop, storage, and photography studio. (Photo by Esther B. Colcord)

Above: January 1985 found the Belleview Biltmore packed as sports enthusiasts checked in for Super Bowl XVIII. One of the festivities celebrating this sports phenomenon called for using a Jeep as a centerpiece in the Starlight Room. (Photo from the Belleview Mido Collection)

the agreement permitting Belleview Biltmore guests to use the courses expired.

The next six months were filled with legal wrangles, but by the end of the year, Powell was once again operating the Belleview Biltmore.

And so matters continued until September of 1989 when Hideo Kurosawa saw the Belleview Biltmore for the first time. His reaction was immediate and ended his six-year search for an American investment. "I thought it was a castle, a palace," Kurosawa is quoted as saying. "It's a place where you can feel the history.'

On April 26, 1990, Kurosawa bought the Belleview Biltmore, the Belleview Biltmore Cabana Club or Sand Key, and the Pelican Country Club, an eighteen-hole, 72-par,

The west lobby which served the guests for nearly a century now houses an art gallery and restaurant, the Terrace Cafe, and is still one of the busiest areas of the hotel. Today, of course, it is filled with guests browsing through the selection of objets d'art in the art gallery and wandering down the main corridor which has a newsstand/gift shop and several apparel stores. (Photo from the Belleview Mido Collection)

Donald Ross–designed golf course a mile from the hotel. The price tag for the properties was $27.5 million.

Kurosawa began an extensive program of expansion and renovation. An avid golfer, it was natural that one of his first projects would be the construction of a new, Victorian-style clubhouse for the Pelican Country Club. It has since been renamed the Belleview Mido Country Club and the hotel renamed the Belleview Mido Resort Hotel, taking the name *Mido* from Kurosawa's corporation in Japan.

Kurosawa's other renovations included the construction of a new lobby on the east side of the hotel providing handicap accessibility unavailable from the old lobby; four all-weather new red-clay tennis

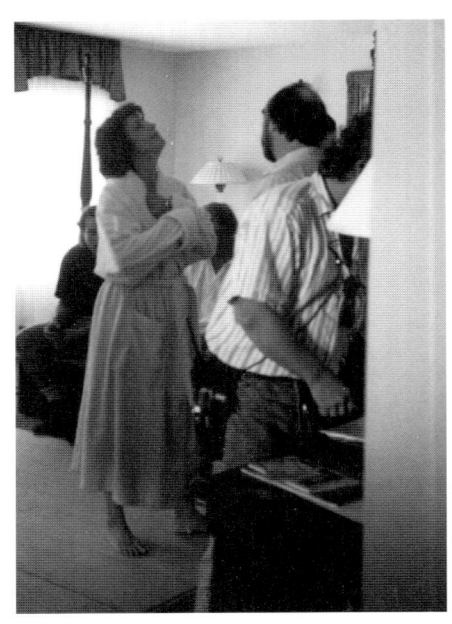

courts; a swimming pool to replace the original pool which had fallen into disrepair; the three-bedroom, 3,400–square foot luxurious Presidential Suite and restoration of many guest rooms.

The Belleview Mido opened to the public in November of 1991. The years since have been kind and once again, the Belleview Mido's future is secure. She is owned by a man who truly appreciates what she represents. Kurosawa says, "The Belleview Mido exists after overcoming numerous difficulties for long periods of time. She is history and tradition. She gives people courage and a rare sense of excitement about life." The Belleview Mido's second century promises to be every bit as exciting and fulfilling as the first. Her guests will fill her registers with home addresses from exotic areas of the world as she moves into the twenty-first century and an international market. But she'll remain the same . . . a regal Southern belle dispensing hospitality with grace and warmth.

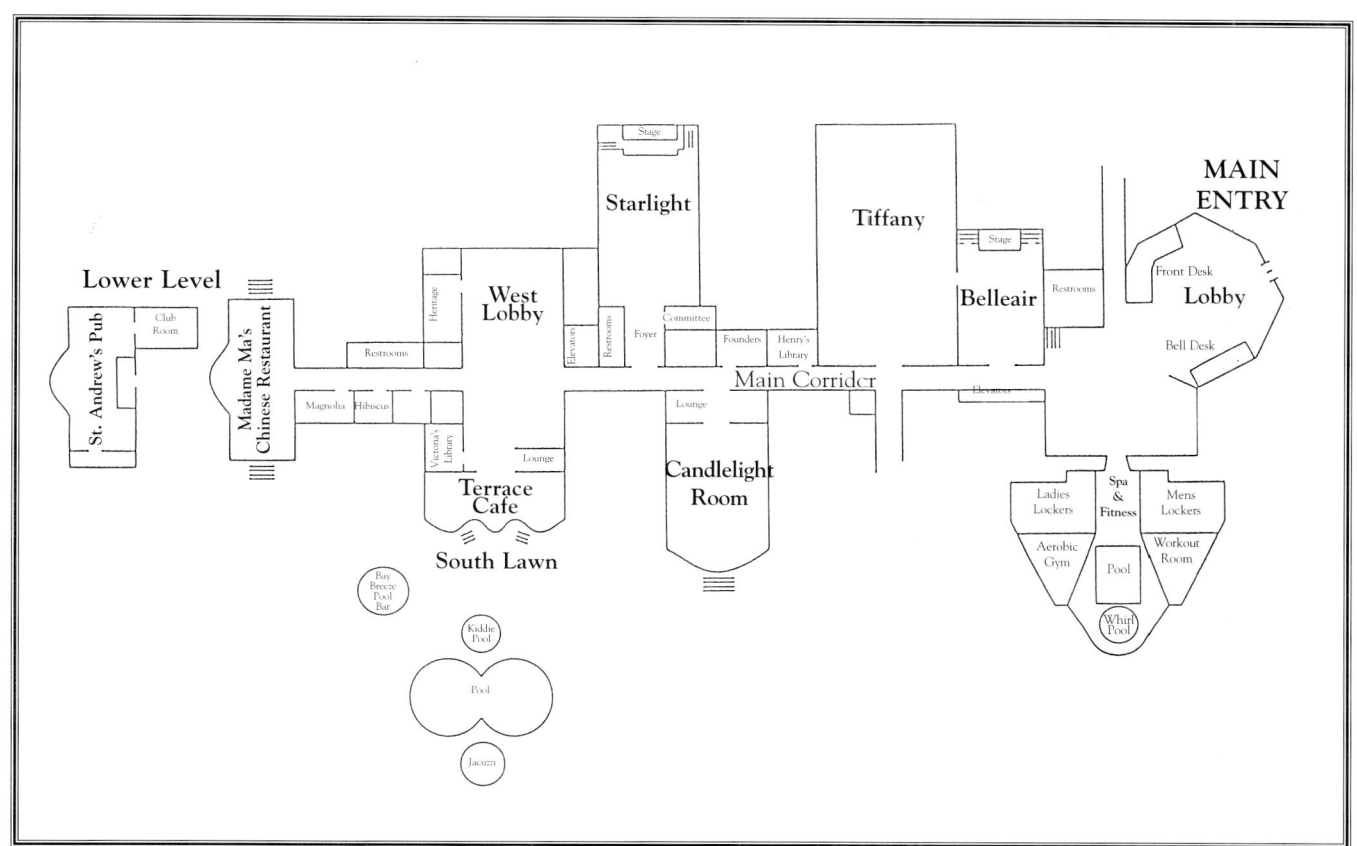

Facing page: The Belleview Mido became a television star in the fall of 1995 when used as a backdrop for the filming of a segment of ABC-TV's family drama entitled "Second Noah." These technicians were installed in a room in the Presidential Suite while in the next room, actress Betsy Brantley who plays the female lead, Jesse Beckett, reacts to the news that—in the script—her TV children are threatened by a hurricane. (Photos by Prudy Taylor Board)

Above: A map of the Belleview Mido's first floor.(From the Belleview Mido Archives)

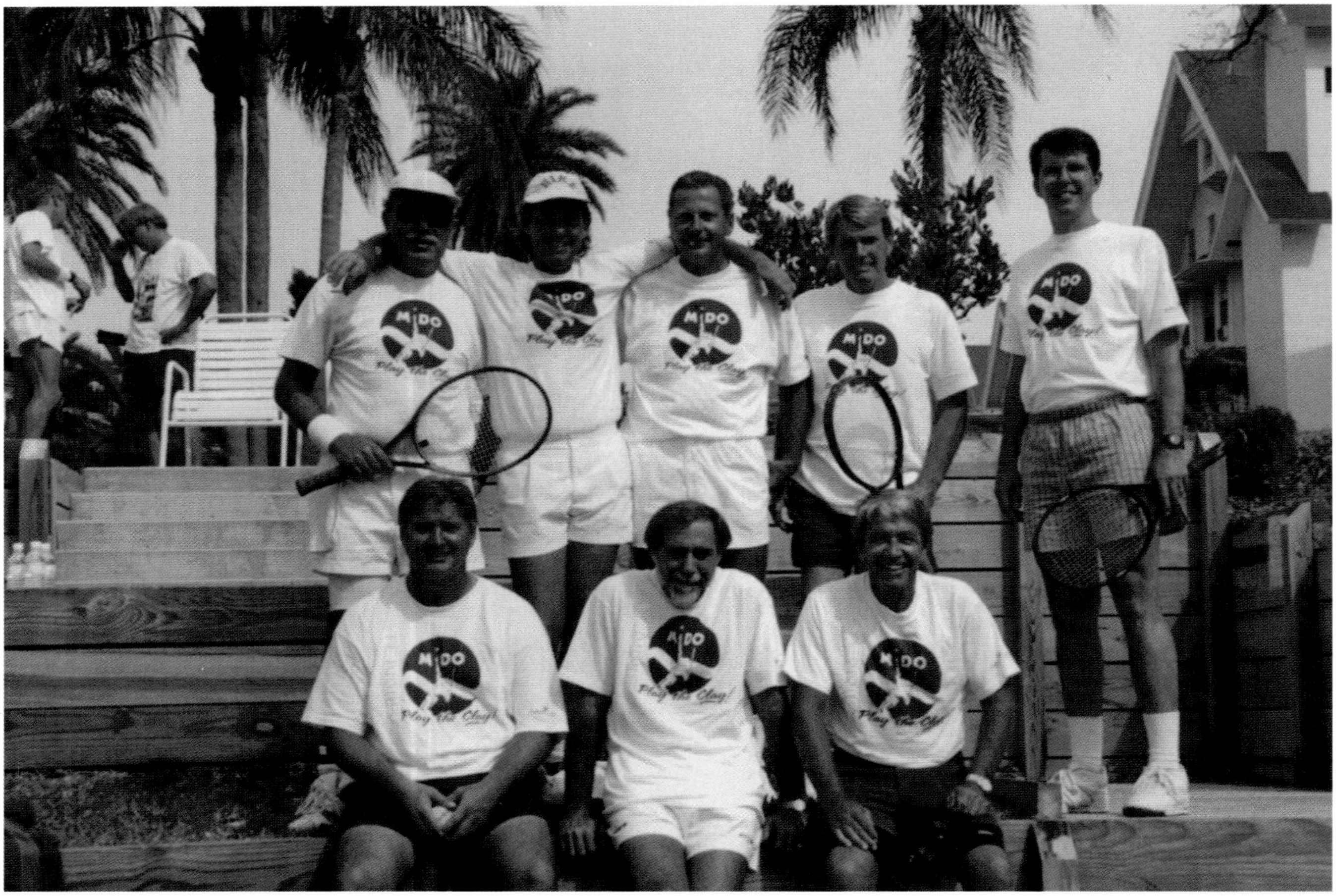

Above: Tennis remains an important sport at the Belleview Mido. Four all-weather red clay courts added as part of the Mido renovation are available for guests. (Photo from the Belleview Mido Collection)

Right: This certificate dated December 26, 1979, officially lists the Belleview Biltmore on the National Register of Historic Places as of December 26, 1979, and attests to the hotel's historic significance. It is displayed in the hotel museum. (From the Belleview Mido Archives)

State of Florida

IN RECOGNITION OF ITS SIGNIFICANCE AND TO ENCOURAGE ITS PRESERVATION

Belleview-Biltmore Hotel

IS HEREBY OFFICIALLY LISTED ON

The National Register of Historic Places

OFFICE OF ARCHAEOLOGY AND HISTORIC PRESERVATION
HERITAGE CONSERVATION AND RECREATION SERVICE
DEPARTMENT OF THE INTERIOR
WASHINGTON, D.C.

ENTERED ON December 26, 1979

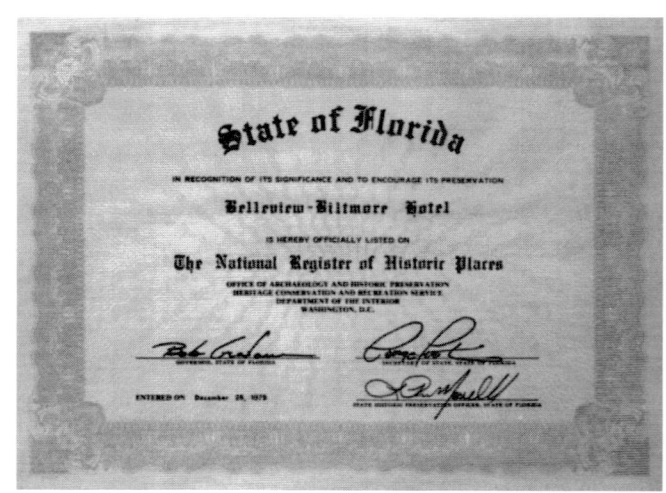

Left: Another brush with television fame occurred in February 1993 when professional wrestler Hulk Hogan announced in a press conference at the Belleview Mido that he would star in a two-hour pilot for CBS entitled "Thunder In Paradise." The series, now aired on WTBS, is filmed at different sites in Pinellas County. (Photo from the Belleview Mido Collection)

Below: On April 26, 1990, Hideo Kurosawa (standing), president of Mido Development Company Ltd., and Bernard F. Powell (seated next to Kurosawa) finalized the purchase and sale of the Belleview for $27.5 million. "It's a place where you can feel the history," Kurosawa said. "When I saw this hotel for the first time, I was very moved and attracted by the elegant charm of the historic building." (Photo courtesy of Heritage Village)

June 1993 was a tumultuous month for the Belleview Mido. At 5:00 a.m. on Friday the eleventh, the night auditor noticed that Brightwater, the historic cottage built by the Jacob Disston family, was in flames. Caused by a lightning strike, the fire was so intense firefighting units from five departments took two hours to bring it under control. The destruction was complete and the loss valued between $250,000 and $500,000 although the historic loss could never be valued in dollars. (Photo courtesy of Flo Zimmerman and the Belleair Bee)

Around dinnertime on Monday, June 14, 1993, a tornado touched down uprooting this tree on the perimeter of the Belleview Mido Country Club. Thirty-two additional trees on the course were toppled. Fortunately, no structural damage was suffered and the first nine holes were closed but only temporarily. (Photo courtesy of Flo Zimmerman)

Above: A major item on the list of proposed renovations was the construction of a new swimming pool on the south lawn. The original pool built in 1917 was leaking nearly one thousand gallons of water a day. Kurosawa filled in the pool and constructed the contoured pool with Whirlpool and children's pool shown above. (Photo from the Belleview Mido Collection)

Left: The items on the menu have changed over the years; however, the kitchen still bustles with activity depending on the time of day much as it did a hundred years ago. Gleaming pots and pans line the shelves. The aromas of roasting meats and simmering vegetables fill the air and the chef's staff, wearing appropriate hats, labors to maintain the Belleview Mido's reputation for good food and excellent service. (Photo by Esther B. Colcord)

Above: Belleview Mido Maintenance Supervisor Gary Larson displays one of the bellmen's uniforms stored on the fifth floor. The rack of uniforms represents a mini history of style, but one of the more recent uniforms is on display in the museum. (Photo by Esther B. Colcord)

This telephone booth on the first floor was constructed in 1925. The booth, a delightful remnant of the past, is equipped with a modern phone and provides the caller with a degree of privacy not available in today's modular wall units. (Photo by Esther B. Colcord)

Above: "Frances," the Belleview's LaFrance fire engine, no longer responds to emergency calls. Today she is housed at Heritage Village and used for parades and special events in town and at the Belleview. Fireman Chris Sipiora, shown here with Frances, takes good care of her. Sipiora, along with volunteers from the Belleair Fire Department, worked hard to raise $7,000 to buy her from Mike Morris in 1990. Morris, a retired fireman from the Pittsburgh (Pennsylvania) Fire Department, found her in front of a furniture store in Tarpon Springs in 1970. He and his wife bought her for $950 and began the restoration. The Belleview's sister truck is owned by movie actress June Allyson and is in a museum in California. (Photo by Esther B. Colcord)

Above: Checkers, coloring books, ping pong dominos—there has always been something for the youngest guests to do. (Photo from the Belleview Mido Collection)

Above: This original entrance, located at the west side of the hotel, opened into the main lobby. Porches with fanlights, intricate molding, and rails dominated the area. The covered entranceway provided shelter from inclement weather for carriages and later for cars. (Photo courtesy of Flo Zimmerman)

Right: The Belleview Mido's corridors span two miles, use six miles of carpet, and reveal much about the hotel. The colors, the patterns, the chandeliers in the decor all bespeak the Victorian era. The pipe in the ceiling, however, is part of the sprinkler system installed by the U.S. Army Air Corps. The Belleview Mido has never experienced a major fire, but the sprinklers are routinely maintained and would function effectively. (Photo from the Belleview Mido Collection)

Facing page: The entrance to the Belleview Mido is landscaped with tropical plantings. (Photo from the Belleview Mido Collection)

The breakfast buffet features fresh tropical fruits in season and Danish and French pastries, coffeecakes, bagels, and breads baked from scratch in the Belleview Mido's kitchens. The chefs stand ready to serve the guests. (Photo from the Belleview Mido Collection)

Facing page, above right: The grand opening hosted by the Belleview Mido in November 1991 attracted a crowd of nearly ten thousand. The new octagonal lobby was packed with guests, dignitaries, and the media. Champagne flowed freely, piano music filled the air along with the chatter of conversation. Food tents on the south lawn served all day long. (Photo from the Belleview Mido Collection)

Facing page; left: The children's dining room has been redecorated and today is the scene of small meetings. (Photo from the Belleview Mido Collection)

Above: Opened in March 1987, this exercise room was part of the 12,000–square foot spa and the $7 million restoration of the interior done by the Belleview Biltmore Associates Ltd., a new management partnership that took over operation of the hotel in 1985. The original partners were Charles Rutenberg, Salu Devnani, and Chris Reyelt. (Photo from the Belleview Mido Collection)

Left: An aerial view of the contoured pool. The new pool on the south lawn is three times the size of the original, contains two hundred thousand gallons of water and is the largest hotel pool in Pinellas County. (Photo from the Belleview Mido Collection)

Below: Opening the same day as the Belleview Mido in 1991 was Madam Ma's, an elegant Chinese restaurant named after its owner Nancy Chih Ma on the left in this photo. Madam Ma is internationally known for her Chinese cuisine. The woman on the right is her daughter-in-law Irene. (Photo from the Belleview Mido Collection)

The view from the south lawn. Although its environs have been transformed due to the area's incredible development, the Belleview Mido is much the same as when she first opened in 1897. The hotel is more comfortable— air conditioning was added in 1972 and 1973. Other improvements have been made through the decades. However, the Belleview Mido remains "The White Queen of the Gulf," a Southern lady dispensing hospitality with grace, elegance, and warmth. (Photo from the Belleview Mido Collection)

From the air, the Belleview Mido looks much the same as it did a century ago. (Photo from the Belleview Mido Collection)

CHAPTER FIVE

Through the Years in Color

Another view of the new entrance revealing the columns of bronze-tinted glass and mirrors surrounded by reflecting pools. (Photo from the Belleview Mido Collection)

The new lobby with its abundance of glass is ablaze with light which is reflected by an aluminum chandelier especially designed for the Belleview Mido. Local historians complained the new lobby looked like a series of pagodas. Once the construction was completed, the community was reassured. The lobby was also designed to save two historic oaks over two hundred years old which can be seen through the lobby's windows. (Photo from the Belleview Mido Collection)

An artist's rendering of the new entrance.
(Photo from the Belleview Mido Collection)

Above: The grand opening of the Belleview Mido in November of 1991 was a happy occasion marked with clowns, mimes, magicians, and music. (Photo from the Belleview Mido Collection)

Right: Memories on display. These bingo cards and bright balls, relics from the Belleview Mido's past, are among the colorful exhibits in the museum on the first floor. (Photo by Esther B. Colcord)

Facing page: At the lectern, new owner Hideo Kurosawa talked of the hotel's past and his plans for the future. (Courtesy of Heritage Village)

Right: The ribbon cutting at the grand opening brought smiles from Mr. Kurosawa and Belleair Mayor Ned Moran (right foreground). (Photo from the Belleview Mido Collection)

Above: The view from the fifth floor reveals timeless tropical beauty. (Photo from the Belleview Mido Collection)

Left: The Belleview Mido's corridors that today reverberate with the sights and sounds of the 1990s were once filled with dignified gentlemen with mutton chop whiskers and elegant ladies in long skirts bearing parasols who strolled to the strains of waltz music.(Photo by Esther B. Colcord)

Facing page: The hotel's south porch provides many examples of the architectural elements that make the Belleview Mido both historic and charming. Since this photo was taken, the Terrace Patio and pool have been added. (Belleview Mido Collection)

Golfers are still very much a part of the Belleview Mido scene. (Photo from the Belleview Mido Collection)

Tennis remains a favorite pastime at the Belleview Mido. There are now four red clay tennis courts on which to play. (Photo from the Belleview Mido Collection)

Left: Azure water, verdant greens, and a backdrop of swaying palms created a tropical paradise for these golfers before the Belleview Mido Country Club opened. (Photo from the Belleview Mido Collection)

Below: Pool fun. Note the beautiful tile work in this photo of the original pool Morton Plant built in 1917. (Photo from the Belleview Mido Collection)

Facing page, left: Part of the Biltmore Hotel Association's $10 million renovation plan called for the refurbishing of the guest rooms. As evidenced by this photo, the Victorian decor and ambiance has been retained and enhanced. (Photo from the Belleview Mido Collection)

Right: Mr. Hideo Kurosawa. While attending Waseda University where he received a BA in Law, Kurosawa founded Mido Development Corporation Ltd. Now headquartered in Osaka, Japan, the company is capitalized $48 million and has approximately 750 employees worldwide. The Belleview Mido is the company's only property in the United States. (Photo courtesy of Mido Development Corporation Ltd.)

Left: Nooks and niches, porches, and patios provide the Belleview Mido's guests with relaxing hideaways. (Photo by Esther B. Colcord)

Below: Today the grounds of the Belleview Mido serve as a backdrop not only for lawn parties, Easter egg hunts, and concerts, but also more and more local brides are choosing to have their functions including the wedding ceremony at the hotel. (Photo from the Belleview Mido Collection)

This historic oak which graces the Belleview Mido's lawn made history in the field of forestry. Several years ago, the tree was dying. Foresters from the University of Florida brought massive hypodermic needles and dosed this tree with gargantuan injections of antibiotics. The treatment was successful as is evidenced here. (Photo courtesy of Flo Zimmerman)

Bibliography

BOOKS AND PAMPHLETS

Bruccoli, Matthew J., ed. *Ring Around the Bases*. New York: Charles Scribner's Sons and Macmillan Publishing Co., 1992.

Dictionary of American Biography. Vol. 7, pp. 646–647.

Fountain, Charles. *Sportswriter: The Life and Times of Grantland Rice*. New York: Oxford University Press, 1993.

Harner, Charles E. *Florida's Promoters*. Tampa, Fla.: Trend House, n.d.

Henry B. Plant Museum staff. *Moments In Time*. Promotional booklet.

"Henry Bradley Plant and Florida." *Florida Historical Quarterly*, October 1966

Historic Preservation Certification Application: Part I- Evaluation of Significance; Part II-Certification Application. Submitted by Christopher J. Reyelt, general manager, August 25, 1985.

Historical Background of Belleview prepared by Pinellas County Planning Department. N.d.

Morris, Allen, comp. *The Florida Handbook 1991–1992*, 23rd Biennial Edition, Tallahassee, Fla.: The Peninsular Publishing Co.

Muir, Helen. *The Biltmore Hotel*. Miami, Fla.: The Pickering Press, 1987.

National Cyclopaedia of American Biography. Vol 18., pp. 286–287

Perez, Patricia. *American History Project: The Belleview-Biltmore Hotel*. Pinellas Historical Commission, 1964.

Salamanca, Lucy Nuttall. *Belleair the Alluring*. St. Petersburg, Fla.: Tourist News Press, n.d.

MAGAZINES

Burke, John O. "White Queen of the Gulf." *Suncoast Magazine*, November 12, 1984.

"Golfing Landmark of the Gulf Coast, The." *The Florida Golfer*, July 1974.

Menge, Eric E. "Our Florida Heritage." *Florida Living*, November 1994.

NEWSPAPERS

"A Grand Time at the Belleview Hotel." *The Bee/Leader*, November 11, 1991.

Aland, Beverly J. "Changes to Hotel Are Criticized by Historic Panels." *The Bee/Leader*, October 18, 1990.

Albury, Chuck. "Belleview Biltmore Hotel Opens Season." *Clearwater Times*, January 9, 1983.

_____. "Belleview Biltmore Opens for Its 83rd Season." *Largo-Seminole Times*, January 7, 1979.

_____. "Belleview Biltmore Opens Season Today." *St. Petersburg Times*, 1981.

_____. "Belleview Biltmore Opens Today." *St. Petersburg Times*, January 1969.

_____. "Belleview Biltmore to Begin Its 86th Winter Season Monday." *Clearwater Times*, January 9, 1982.

_____. "Belleview Biltmore." *St. Petersburg Times*, January 9, 1983.

_____. "Belleview Hotel's 88th Season Opens Tuesday." *Largo/Seminole Times*, January 1985.

_____. "Clearwater Man Logs Year's Aid." *St. Petersburg Times*, December 1971.

_____. "Good Morning" column. *St. Petersburg Times*, January 1972.

_____. "The Day That Golfing Great Hagen's Charm Melted Butter." *St. Petersburg Times*, March 13, 1979.

_____. "U.S. Steel Buys Land at Sand Key, Belleair." *St. Petersburg Times*, August 13, 1969.

Atkins, Eric. "Huge Hotel Built in '95 by Henry Plant." *Clearwater Sun*, 1962 Mailaway Edition.

_____. "Posh Belleview Biltmore has Colorful History." *Clearwater Sun*, October 26, 1962.

"Beautiful and Enterprising Belleair." *West Hillsborough Press*, Illustrated Edition, 1900/1901.

"Belleview Biltmore Gets Okay to Build Spa." *Clearwater Sun*, n.d.

"Belleview Biltmore Sets Flag Raising." *St. Petersburg Times*, January 8, 1972.

"Belleview Biltmore to Open Season January 6th." *St. Petersburg Times*, December 30, 1972.

Benbow, Charles. "White Queen of the Gulf Continues to Reign, The." *St. Petersburg Times*, August 20, 1987.

_____. "'White Queen of the Gulf' Still Puts Guests in Awe." *St. Petersburg Times*, January 1981.

Bertke, Roy. "U.S. Steel's Sand Key Buy For $10 million Now Official." *Tampa Tribune*, October 10, 1969.

Bothwell, Dick. "All Things Owed." *St. Petersburg Times*, n.d.

_____. "Hotel That Time Forgot, The." *St. Petersburg Times*, January 27 and 28, 1973.

_____. "Journey Into The Past." *St. Petersburg Times*, January 15, 1969.

Byrne, Maureen. "Belleview Mido Cottage Burns." *Bellair Bee*, June 17, 1993.

———. "Boxing Makes a Punch at Hotel." *Belleair Bee*, September 24, 1992.

———. "Step Back in Time." *Belleair Bee*, December 17, 1992.

———. "'Thunder' Rolls Onto the Suncoast." *Belleair Bee*, February 25, 1993.

Clarke, Jay. "Style Remains at Grand Hotels of Florida's Heyday." *Philadelphia Inquirer*, January 28, 1979.

"Clearwater and Sand Key to Share Sewage Plant." *St. Petersburg Times*. August 15, 1969."

Cosdon, Christina K. "An Old Hotel Checks in Among Nation's History." *St. Petersburg Times*, March 8, 1980.

Costa, Margery. "Splashy New Spa Continues Elite Tradition of Resort," *Clearwater Sun*, March 2, 1987.

"Dionne Warwick Entertains 400 Attendance." *The Bee*, January 21, 1993.

Dorris, Tony. "Hotel Battles." *St. Petersburg Times*, June 7, 1987.

———. "Hotel Wins a Needed Victory." *St. Petersburg Times*, January 8, 1988.

Foxwell, Tish. "Hotel Belleview Biltmore." *St. Petersburg Times*, March 23, 1986.

Froelich, Janis D. "Taking lunch at the Belleview Biltmore." *St. Petersburg Times*, November 10, 1986.

Goodgame, Bettie Wilder. "History of the Town of Belleair: Belleair Abandoned Then Reborn." *Belleair Breeze*, September 1975.

Gray, Ruth. "The Belleview Biltmore Offers Elegant Dining." *St. Petersburg Times*, n.d.

Greiff, James. "Resort for Well-heeled." *St. Petersburg Times*, April 27, 1987.

Harper, Philip. "Elegant White Queen Bows to Change." *Clearwater Sun*, January 21, 1979.

Harris, Bonnie. "Murder! Ordinary People Turn Detective." *St. Petersburg Times*, n.d.

"IRB Broker Files Suit Over Sand Key Sales." *St. Petersburg Times*, 1969.

Kent, Marge Costa. "Belleview Biltmore Glitters for Thousands." *Belleair Bee*, November 7, 1991.

"Last Vestiges of a Picturesque Empire." Heritage column by *Clearwater Sun* staff writers.

"More Than the Lobby Is Unsettling." *St. Petersburg Times*, August 8, 1991.

Moritsugu, Ken, and Lewis, Rochelle D. "Japanese Developer Buys Belleview Biltmore." *St. Petersburg Times*, April 27, 1990.

"Old Hotel Retains Charm: The Glories of Early Florida." *Fort Lauderdale News*, January 20, 1969.

"Old Warhorse Hopes to Settle in Belleair." *Belleair Bee/Leader*, October 30, 1986.

Pallasch, Abdon M. "Historic Homes Fail to Stand the Test of Time." *Tampa Tribune*, October 30, 1992.

"Partnership Leases Belleview Biltmore." *St. Petersburg Times*, December 1985.

"Plant's New Paradise." Tampa, Fla.: *Weekly Tribune, The*, Vol. 4, No. 28, Thursday, August 26, 1896.

"Powell Speaking to Belleair Commissioners." *The Bee/Leader*, August 28, 1986.

Pyros, John. "Former Tarpon High Star to Face WBO Boxing Champ." *Tarpon Springs Leader*, October 2, 1992.

Sanders, Mike. "Casa Mia History: A Chronicle of the Day." *Belleair Bee*, Bee Publications, June 1987.

"Spectacular Piece of Americana Is One for the Books." *St. Petersburg Times*, January 1977.

Stidham, Joseph. "Belleview Biltmore Resort Changes Hands." *Tampa Tribune*, n.d.

"U.S. Steel Agrees To Buy Prime Gulf Coast Property." *Wall Street Journal*, August 14, 1969.

"U.S. Steel Condominium Plans Clarify." *Bellair Breeze*, August 1971.

"U.S. Steel's Belleair Site Plans." *Belleair Breeze*, November 1972."

Whitney, Elizabeth. "Broker Contends He's Salvaged $11 million Sale of Sand Key." *St. Petersburg Times*, October 8, 1969.

———. "Proposal is for U.S. Steel is Just That." *St. Petersburg Times*, October 9, 1969.

Wright Countersuit is filed." *St. Petersburg Times*, October 31, 1969.

Yeomans, Marty. "Tiny Island's Bridge Is Coming Down." *Clearwater Sun*, March 16, 1987.

BROCHURES

Belleview and Cottages, The. New York: F. W. Robinson, circa 1908.

Bernard F. and Mary Ann Powell Cancer Pavilion at the Morton F. Plant Hospital, The. Program from dedication ceremony, July 29, 1995.

Brief Bio of Donald J. Ross. Courtesy of Donald J. Ross Foundation.

"Henry B. Plant Museum." "Henry 'Planted' Seeds for Growth in the South." *Tampa Tribune*, n.d.

Raymond, H. H. *Pinellas Country Club*, 192_.

NEWSLETTERS

Belleair Newsletter, The. Belleair Property Owners Association, November 1962.

"Belleview Biltmore: A Repeat Visit to the Grande Dame, The." *Alcoa Contractor News*, 1985.

Index

A
Adams Express, 12
Ade, George, 22
administrative staff, 64, 84
air conditioning, 104
Alexander, Captain, 73
Allyson, June, 97
aluminum siding, 84
American LaFrance fire engine, 27, 97
Antique shop, 17
art gallery, 89
Astaire, Fred, 72
Atlantic Coast Line Railroad, 16, 30

B
Baltimore and Ohio Railroad, 39
barber shop, 19
bathing pavilion, 18
Baumann, Gustav, 43
Bayou, The (cottage), 36
Beach and Cabana Club, 82
Beach, Rex, 34, 38
Beckett, Jesse, 91
Belleair, 14, 27, 42, 55, 63
Belleair Breeze, 62
Belleair Country Club, 86
Belleair Fire Department, 27, 63, 97
Belleview, 7, 14, 19, 21, 28, 30
Belleview Biltmore Associates Ltd., 101
Belleview Biltmore Cabana Club, 89
Belleview Biltmore Country Club, 38
Belleview Biltmore Hotel, 22, 34, 35, 36, 37, 38, 39, 40–41, 42, 43, 45, 47, 52, 54, 55, 56, 57, 60, 61, 62, 63, 64, 66, 69, 70–71, 72, 74, 75, 76, 77, 79, 82, 84, 86, 89, 92
Belleview Mido Country Club, 89, 94, 118
Belleview Mido Resort Hotel, 12, 25, 37, 70–71, 78, 84, 85, 87, 89, 90, 91, 92, 93, 94, 96, 98, 101, 102, 104, 106, 110, 116, 117, 120–121
"Belleview Waltz, The," 28
bellmen's uniforms, 96
Belmont Hotel, 43
Bennett, Constance, 35
bicycle racing, 19
bicycle shop, 88
bicycle track, 12
bicycling, 2, 10, 15, 21
billiards, 19
Biltmore Hotel Association, 112, 121
Biltmore Hotel chain, 22, 34, 39
Bimini Room, 81
Blackstone, Ellen Elizabeth, 16
boat dock, 18
Bolton, George, 21
Boston Braves, 44
Boston Red Sox, 44
Bower, Byrne, 46
Bower, Byrne, Mrs., 46
bowling alley, 88
Bowman Hotels, 48, 49
Bowman, John McEntee, 22, 34, 36, 39, 43
Brantley, Betsy, 91
breakfast buffet, 100
Brightwater (cottage), 37, 66, 94
Brooklyn Dodgers, 42, 44
Butler, Nick, 21

C
Cabana and Beach Club, 75
Cabana Club, 45, 54, 75
Candlelight Room, 76
Cartier's, 29
Casa Mia (cottage), 38
Case, Karin, 85
Cedar Key, 14
Center Cemetery, 12
chandeliers, 47, 87, 98, 108
Chicago White Sox, 42
children, 26, 27, 65, 68, 69, 73, 74, 75, 77, 95, 97, 101
Church, Donald, 58, 60, 64, 79
Cincinnati Reds, 42
citrus groves, 14, 21
City National Bank, 39
Clearwater, 15, 18, 52
Clearwater Bay, 16, 27, 45, 82
Clearwater Beach, 61
Cobb, Irvin S., 22
cocktail hour, 46
Coco Plum Beach, 43
Coe's Casino, 36, 54
Coe, William, 54
Cola (fishing launch), 73
Collett, Glenna, 34
color scheme, 25
Comiskey, Charles, 38
concerts, 19, 22
conventions, 86
Coral Gables, 43
corridors, 98, 114, 115
Counts, Patricia, 85
croquet, 22, 77
Culpepper, Ed, Reverend, 21
Curio shop, 17
cyclists, 27

D
Davis Cup, 79
Dembeck, Joseph, 62
Depression, 56
Devnani, Salu, 86, 101
Didrickson, Babe, 22
dining room, 23, 34, 42, 47, 74, 112, 113
Disston, Jacob, 37, 66, 94
dormitory, 34, 50–51, 73
Drew Air Field, 42
Duke of Windsor, 54, 58, 63
Duke of Windsor Suite, 58
Dunham, Edna, 35
DuPont family, 34

E
East Gate Cottage, 37
east basement, 88
east course, 45, 63
east wing, 20, 23, 25
Easter Egg Hunt, 74
Edison, Thomas, 28
Eldridge, J. J., 14
Empire State Building, 60
entrance, 40, 63, 98, 99
entrance bridge, 17, 52–53
entrance, new, 108, 109
Evening Star (sailing vessel), 14

F
Farrell, Johnny, 44
fire department, 27, 42
fishing, 18, 19, 22, 54, 72
flag ceremony, 42
flag raising, 74
Fleming, W. J., 15
Flynn, Charles, 43
Ford, Henry, 28
Fort Myers, 14
Fort Myers Hotel, 36
Fox, Donna, 73
Franke, Dave, 78
fresh water spring, 31

G
Gaylorde, Michael, 67, 68, 69
General Electric, 79
Gilford, Cal, 61
Gilpin, Lucy Disston, 66
golf courses, 14, 15, 18, 19, 20, 22, 25, 26, 27, 34, 38, 42, 44, 45, 48, 49, 52, 57, 58, 60, 61, 63, 69, 84, 86, 89, 94, 116–117, 118–119
Gourdin, Robert, 85
Graham, Billy, 54
grand opening (1991), 101, 110, 111
grand staircase, 85
Green, Ray E., 18
Gremlin, The (fishing launch), 72
Grimm, Marion, 66
Griswold Hotel, 43
grounds, 24, 39, 45, 66, 99, 102, 121
guest rooms, 90, 120, 121
Guggenheim, Meyer, 54
Gulf of Mexico, 45

H
Hagen, Walter, 34
handicapped access, 87
Har-Tru court, 69
Harmon, Tommy, 58
heart of pine lumber, 12, 50
Henry B. Plant House, 19
Henry B. Plant Museum, 14, 16, 17, 23, 28, 29, 30, 35
Heritage Village, 97
Hicks, Betty, 34
historic oaks, 108, 122–123
Hogan, Hulk, 93
horse and carriage, 18, 53
horseback riding, 19, 53
Horton, Edward Everett, 72, 73
hospital train car, 15
Hotel Manhattan, 43
House of Cartier, 29
Hoyt family, 38
hunting, 19, 22
hurricanes, 36

I
Intracoastal Waterway, 75

J
Jackson, Roy, 43
Johnson, Charles Wharton, 14
Jones, Bobby, 22, 34

K
K Corporation, 39
K Natus Corporation, 39
Kelleher, R. T., 79
Kennard, Francis J., 14, 16
Kennedy Performing Arts Center, 60
King, Marjorie, 35
Kirkeby, Arnold, 39, 42, 45, 47
Kirkeby Hotel, 39, 42
Kissimmee Hotel, 36
kitchen, 23, 95
kitchen staff, 64, 80

Kugler, Oliver, 84
Kurosawa, Hideo, 89, 90, 93, 95, 111, 121
L
LaFrance fire engine, 97
Landis, Kennesaw M., Judge, 22, 34, 42
landscaping, 21
Lardner, Ring, 52
Largo Lions Club, 27
Larson, Gary, 96
lawn, northwest, 24
Lee, Robert E., 14
Life magazine, 45
little red schoolhouse, 66, 77
livery stable, 19
Lizak, Lisa, 62
lobby, 13, 98
lobby, new, 87, 89, 101, 108
Loughman, Margaret Josephine, 16
luncheon menu, 25
M
Ma, Nancy Chih, 103
MacDill Air Field, 42
Madam Ma's, 103
Magnavox Corporation, 39
Magnolia (cottage), 37
main entrance, 31
Manwaring, Maisie Cadwell, 29
map of first floor, 91
Martin, Jeffry, 84, 85
Marzard, Rube, 44
Mascotte, S.S., 23
McAlpin, Scotty, 65
McElmurry, Argie, 87
McFarland, Beber, Mrs., 46
McKenzie, Dickie, Miss, 21
Merrick, George E., 43
Meza, Mike, 84
Miami Biltmore, 43
Mido Development Corporation 87, 93, 121
Miller, Michael J., 14, 16
Mobil Travel Guide, 86
Moet Chandon, 85
Moore, Kathleen, 84
Moran, Ned, Mayor, 111
Morris, Mike, 97
Morton F. Plant Hospital, 15, 20
movies, 78
Murray Hill Hotel, 43
museum, 17, 92, 96, 110
N
National Register of Historic Places, 7, 86, 92
New York Giants, 44
New York Yankees, 44
Newman, J. W., 14
newsstand, 19

newsstand/gift shop, 89
Notre Dame, 52
O
Oakley Country Club, 22
Ocala House (hotel), 36
Olivette, S.S., 23
Orange Belt Railroad, 19
orchestra, 13, 19
Ouimet, Francis, 34
P
painting maintenance, 84
Palm Cottage, 20
Palmer, Arnold, 38
Peabody, Nora, 60, 64
Peck, Gregory, 38
Peebles, Mrs., 77
Peerless Magnarc (movie projector), 78
Pelican Country Club, 89
Peninsular and Occidental Steamship Company, 30
Pergola and Tea House, 51
Pew family, 34
photography studio, 88
Pinellas County, 93, 103
Pinellas County Historical Museum, 12, 66
Plant, Ellen, 12
Plant Family Genealogy, 30
Plant, H. B., Mrs., 28
Plant, Henry B., 7, 12, 14, 17, 25, 26, 27, 28, 30, 36
Plant, Henry B., II, 15, 20, 36
Plant Investment Company, 14, 19, 34
Plant, Maisie Cadwell Manwearing, 29, 35
Plant, Morton Freeman, 12, 14, 15, 19, 20, 25, 20, 22, 25, 29, 34, 35
Plant, Philip Manwaring, 29, 35
Plant steamship line, 23, 30
Plant System, The (railroads), 14, 28
police department, 27, 42
post office, 28, 42
Powell, Bernard F., 58, 60, 64, 65, 75, 84, 86, 93
Powell, Kathy, 73
Powell, Mary, 60
power plant, 42
Power, Tyrone, 36, 54
Presidential Suite, 90, 91
Pullman cars, 15
R
railroads, 14, 15, 16, 17, 19, 28, 30, 34, 76, 88
Railway Express Company, 30
real estate market, 36

renovations, 60, 88, 89, 95, 101, 121
Reyelt, Christopher, 86, 101
Rice, Grantland, 34, 52
Richards, J. R., 56
Ritchie, James H., 34
Rogers, Flossie, Miss, 21
Rogers, Fred, 38
Rogers, Ginger, 72, 73
Ross, Donald J., 18, 20, 22, 89
Rutenberg, Charles, 86, 101, 112
Ruth, Babe, 22, 34, 44
S
Saint Patrick's Day, 61
Sand Key, 54, 63, 75, 82, 89
Sand Key Beach, 18
Sarazen, Gene, 34, 44
Seastrom, Paul, 84, 85
"Second Noah," 91
Seminole shell mounds, 15
Seminole, The (hotel), 36
Servos, Launcelot Cressy, 27
shuffleboard, 76
sightseeing, 18, 54
Sipiora, Chris, 97
skeetshooting, 19
Smith, Alex, 34
Smith, MacDonald, 34
Smithsonian Institution, 35
south lawn, 56, 95, 102, 103, 104–105
south porch, 114, 115
south wing, 34
Southern Express Company, 12, 30
Southwest Florida, 17, 30
spa, 86, 101, 112
Spanish-American War, 23
Spurlin, Stella, Miss, 28
St. Andrews Pub, 81, 85
St. Petersburg, 15, 47
St. Petersburg Times, 63
Starlight Room, 61, 72, 73, 78, 89
Stevens, Roger L., 60
Stewart, Burner C, 57
stock market crash, 36, 39
Stone Crab Club, 19, 20
Strong, Kathy Powell, 65, 66
Studebaker family, 34
Studebaker, James, 54
submarine scares, 42, 47
Sunset Cottage, 37
Super Bowl XVIII, 89
swimming pool, 15, 22, 25, 34, 53, 61, 65, 90, 95, 103, 112, 119
T
Tampa, 42
Tampa Bay Hotel, 36
tea garden, 48
telegraph, 19, 28
telephone, 19, 28

telephone booth, 96
tennis, 19, 22, 56, 67, 69, 86, 89, 92, 118
Tennis Shop, 67
Terrace Cafe, 89
Terrace Cottage, 38
Terrace Patio, 115
Thacher, Charles, 75
Thatcher, Margaret, Lady, 85
Themis (statue), 86, 87, 108
"Thunder In Paradise," 93
Tiffany Room, 34, 42, 47, 74
tornado, 94
Trinity College, 54
Turner-Brandon American Legion Post 7, 42, 74
U
U.S. Air Force 672nd Unit Band, 55
U.S. Army Air Corps, 42, 45, 46, 47, 98
U.S. Lawn Tennis Association, 79
U.S. Steel, 63, 79, 82, 84, 86
U.S. Steel Realty Development Corporation, 62
U.S. Supreme court, 60
V
Van Wie, Virginia, 34
Vanderbilt family, 34
verandahs, 16
W
Wall Street Journal, 28
Ware, Richard, Capt., 46
Ware, Richard, Mrs., 46
Warwick Realty, 39
water, 31, 53, 103
water pump, 42
Webster, William, Mrs., 68, 69
west basement, 88
west course, 63
west lobby, 89
west lounge, 44, 45
Whelan, Charles A., 38
White Queen of the Gulf, 7, 12, 19, 60, 63, 102, 104
White, Charles, Mrs., 46
Willard, Daniel, 39
Wilson, Harry J., 57
wine list, 25
Winter Park, 36
wireless, 28
World Tennis Magazine, 86
World War I, 34
World War II, 46, 47, 55, 56, 60
Wright, Ed C., 47, 56, 60, 63, 75
Y
yachting, 19
Z
Ziegler, Hallie, Miss, 21

About the Authors

Prudy Taylor Board, a native of Fort Myers, Florida, and a graduate of the University of Florida, has devoted herself to helping preserve the history of Southwest Florida.

A freelance journalist and novelist, she has had more than a thousand articles published in national and regional magazines, was staff writer for the *Fort Myers News-Press* and managing editor of two regional magazines, *Lee Living* and *Home & Condo*. She also edited *The Fiction Writer*, a magazine for writers distributed nationally.

Her first book, *Lee County: A Pictorial History*, was published by the Donning Company/Publishers in 1985. Her novels, *The Vow* and *Blood Legacy*, were published in 1989 by Leisure Books and Pocket Books. Donning published her most recent books—in 1990, *Pages from the Past: A Pictorial Retrospective of Lee County, Florida*; in 1992, *Historic Fort Myers*; and in 1995, *Venice through the Years: A Pictorial History*. She teaches writing courses at Edison Community College and lectures frequently at writers' conferences around the country.

Esther B. Colcord came to Fort Myers, Florida, in 1946 from Kenmore, New York. She is a graduate of Kenmore High School and has attended Edison Community College.

As a freelance writer, she has long been interested in local history and has had articles printed in local, national, and trade magazines. She has also written book reviews for *The Fiction Writer* magazine. She has authored a children's book entitled *True Tales of Adventure and Mystery in Lee County, Florida* which is composed of factual historical adventures told through the eyes of pioneer children. She coauthored *Pages from the Past* in 1990, *Historic Fort Myers* in 1992, *History of Aviation in Lee County* in 1993, and *Venice through the Years* in 1995. In 1993, she was also coeditor of the Fort Myers Fire Department history entitled *Nine Decades of Service*.

In Fort Myers, she has been active in community affairs, served on the Board of Directors of the Nature Center, as a member of the Southwest Florida Historical Society, and has long been deeply involved in the Edison Pageant of Light and Holiday House. For twelve years, she worked in the travel industry.